# Pebbles

## from Oceanshore of Life

notionpress.com

# Pebbles

## from Oceanshore of Life

Archana Chowdhury

notionpress.com

**Notion Press**

*5, Muthu Kalathy St.*

*Triplicane*

*Chennai – 600005*



*ISBN: 978-93-8380-86-18*

What I have learned, Chance leaps to contradict;
What I have built is seized and torn by Fate
I can foresee the acts of Matter's force,
But not the march of destiny of man;
He is driven upon paths he did not choose,
He falls trampled underneath the rolling wheels.
My great philosophies are a reasoned guess;
The mystic heavens that claim the human soul,
Are a charlatanism of the imagining brain;
All is a speculation or a dream.

**Savitri – Sri. Aurobindo**

*This book is dedicated to My Father*

*Late Prof. Shri Prakritiranjan Barua*

*Who inspired me to take up Medicine*

# About the Author

Archana Chowdhury was born in the state of Maharashtra, India to parents who originally belonged to East Bengal (now Bangladesh). A legacy of academic excellence runs in the families of both her parents. She had a brilliant academic career but was an unwilling entry to the medical curriculum. Obedience, ideology and discipline were genetically ingrained traits, hence there was no revolt against medical education, however reluctant the endeavour might have been. She completed M.B.B.S. and M.D. (Internal Medicine) with excellent academic standing and did Masters in Medical Research Methodology from McMaster University, Hamilton, Canada. Committed to serve fellow human beings and teach students, she joined Maharashtra Medical Education & Research Service.

With vast experience of observing and treating patients from all strata of society, more so the socially marginalized, she persistently evolves her being on yogic principles which are at once transcendental, universal and personal. She regards herself as an ever enthusiastic student, learning from the book of life and existence. Writing is not an endeavour but an expression of realisation, contemplation and meditation for her. With the psyche of a Bengali, spatial orientation, education in Maharashtra, the widening of her mental horizon by travelling to the USA, Canada, Europe, Australia, Asia and blessings from Sri Aurobindo Ashram in Ponchicherry, she consider herself the owner of a blessed life.

# Author's Note

Science and the Art of Medicine is intricately interwoven with life in close vicinity and existence at large making micro to macro-cosm an incessant journey. Learning is a never-ending process in the field of Medicine. Phenotypically so similar, each of us is so different and unique that most generalizations seem superfluous. In every individual there is a special heart that beats, a unique brain that administers, qualitatively different sense organs that function, characteristic sensitivities that nerves carry and disperse, hormones that work without rest and all these perform to make the life-process a success. Above all is the mind with its 'sanskaras', thinking & performance, willpower, intellect that reasons, discerns, discriminates, judges and the soul at the summit which is the sole enjoyer of the total endeavour.

Life is transcendental and universal. At one station that is this life we meet, interact and pass-on. Although, I entered medical school reluctantly, I am convinced of the blessing in disguise. It has been a privileged birth to have been thus placed. Deep is the ocean, but at least I have tasted a dip in its wideness as well as its depth.

# Prologue

One fundamental and intriguing question I have faced is to trace back the point in time when I began learning. The process of learning has always seemed transcendental without beginning and end. The book of life and existence with innumerable hues and fragrance, overtones and undertones, subtleness and vastness is perpetually opening ever new pages from some eternal book of eternity.

This realisation has made of me a constant, enthusiastic and humble pupil of life, although professionally destined to be a medical teacher and a clinician. Learning and the application of knowledge to teach students and to treat patients is very challenging. Teaching and learning is interactive and the roles always interchange and interlace. Patient care learnt from medical books and teachers is the foundation, Montessori education for self-education for a life-time.

The shivers from the dissection room through questioning and examining the first patient independently, to making decisions on one's own for the first time, the anxious time spent in prayer awaiting results of medicines and procedure have paved the way for the professional knowledge as well as insight. Real and true medicine and healing is beyond books and teachers. Each case is unique on the backdrop of a few common features and trends because one sick individual is ill in his own way, with his baggage of genetic & psychological makeup and myriad environmental, social, cultural, and financial factors. Statistical generalizations are futile for a case for whom morbidity or mortality has a specific connotation. The fatality from a disease statistically may be as small as less than two percent but for the patient who dies of the disease it is hundred percent. Health indicators are like medical books for guidance but not for decision-making. The making of a physician from the raw material of a young teenager entering medical school is an educative endeavour for his or her lifetime.

The diagnostic skills developed in bedside learning are supported by aids like various investigations. Investigatory repertoire is expanding in horizon almost every minute in medical research but what is beyond all this is the intuitive intelligence and insight of the treating clinician. In this era of hyperinflation of super specialty, the basis of this tree of knowledge Internal Medicine is suffocating to a great extent. However, that Internal Medicine is the genetic node for the superstructure is undeniable. Internal Medicine as a branch of medical curriculum has a tilt towards gender man. Women doctors opt for Obstetrics & Gynaecology, Ophthalmology, Pathology, Microbiology and other para and pre-clinical specialties. Obediently did I accept to become a physician trusting my father's intuitive visionary ability.

This book is dedicated to the eternal and transcendental flow of life. Events occur like pebbles on its immense shore of myriad hues, shades, forms which disappear like foam but etched are the imprints on the canvas of memory in invisible, indelible ink with finiteness of time and space carrying us forward to realisation of glimpses of the eternal, the universal, the transcendental, yet perceptible, palpable and pulsating in every moment of life. A physician's life is not in years but in days, hours and minutes. Journeying life many a pebble is picked from its vast shore of which a few are here. My heart and soul are thankful to life as my teacher in whichever form, moment and way it is teaching me to live and enjoy living.

# Acknowledgements

My patients (who I refer as cases) have inspired me innocently to delve deep into the phenomenon of life. Late Dr. Vikram Marwah, a surgeon, medical teacher, human par excellence always encouraged me to fulfil my creative urge with colours from canvas of life.

My thanks to Notion Press for publishing my book. My thanks to my computer personnel Prasad Ghotkar and Vidya Mude.

# Contents

## PART I Inspiration and Initiation



## PART II Widening Horizons

## PART IV Colours and Shades of Life

## PART V Technology and Biology

# Part I

## Inspiration and Initiation

*Health is the condition of wisdom and the sign is cheerfulness – an open and noble temper*

*—Ralph Waldo Emerson*

# Case 1

# Prakritiranjan

What is the value of a name? In South India most names are mythologically connected. Names of deities are used frequently if not universally. In Maharashtra proper nouns are used like pronouns without much ado. In Bengal name has a very special place in life. Usually the length is longer to put significant meaning in it. No middle name is used. His name was Prakritiranjan (one who enjoys nature or is ornamental to nature).

In his youth he had a little skepticism about his name as the short form was Prakriti, which connoted feminity to him. His name was off-beat and his being was attuned to his name. He was in rhythm and effusiveness akin to prakriti (nature). In form he was diminutive but titanic in knowledge and courage. Language was his master stroke. Intuitive as he was language, arts, music, dance were closer to his heart. He fathomed science with intuition and not with intellect and analysis. An ace swimmer, an orderly morning walker, once he saw the clock of the General Post Office tower stuck at 5.30. This observation prompted him to write a poem, the gist of which was concept of time. Time and space are the two dimensional units around which the universe revolves. In this small poem beautifully he joined the finite concept of time, created by man to the infinite time.

The season was winter, the year 1995. The weather was cool, and there had been showers for a few days. Habituated to early rising, he followed his routine but that winter was not favourable for him. He caught cold and cough which later worsened to severe bronchitis. Medically, he was deteriorating and hospital admission was unavoidable. There came many volunteers for night duty in his room. One of them was Amit. At that time Amit was working in a hospital with shift duties like any other young doctor, and hence he opted for night duty on a day suitable to him. The whole night, the patient had been restless and Amit took very good care of him. Early next morning as he was sleepy, he said that Amit was a very good person, an excellent doctor and dozed off. Amit returned to his work and told me he would be available on night two days later. Prakritiranjan passed away the following morning at 5.30 a.m. just before dawn. Amit was not required to do another night duty.

Till January, 1995, Amit a very brilliant student with two M.D. degrees and DNB in Medicine was struggling to discover his future. Nothing was working out in a concrete way. Within two months of this event, Amit went to the U.K. for MRCP and now is well placed there with his wonderful wife and two daughters. The interesting story is one of retrospect. Amit had high regards for me as teacher. He discussed almost everything with me. At that time, his parents were looking for girls for him. For this, his father took him to a renowned astrologer who restrained his predictions with discretion and discrimination and did not accept money for his job. When this astrologer saw Amit, he said this young man was a prince in his last birth, had insulted his guru and hence he was destined to become a physician to help the diseased and the dying. This was like a birth for penance.

At dawn after a disturbed night, Prakritiranjan said Amit was a good doctor and a good human being. Amit though very much willing to do night duty again was not required to do so as Prakritiranjan had passed away. Like white steppes in clear space the sojourn of two souls enlightened my inner self. Prakritiranjan was his guru in his last birth and his forgiving broke the occult barriers in Amit's professional career. Amit was released from the shackles of his previous birth to soar high in his medical career.

# Case 2

# Debashish

Dr. Verma (Verma uncle) had come as an external examiner for Zoology to the Institute of Science where my father was a professor of English. He was father's colleague in the previous institution in another city. The association was disrupted due to father's transfer. I was then a medical student, connecting with Dr. Verma after a break of almost ten years; his son Debashish, a year older, was a great friend when we were children in primary school. Verma uncle wished to meet me. Debashish was also studying Medicine.

In a flashback, innocent childhood days flashed in memory. Debashish and I were great pals. Our most favourite place was the swing of the children's park. One sat with legs dangling to give the initial push from ground support, the other stood behind holding the ropes and pushing the swing with bending and straightening from knee and hip joints. We could take the swing very high almost to $30^0$ of the bar on the top from which the swing hung.

It was a rainy day. I had a new green duckback rain coat. With a new raincoat the rains were a welcome happening. Debashish and I went to the swing in the park and were enjoying our plight, but a small danger was lurking somewhere. The swing board was slippery with water and as bad luck Debashish slipped and fell to the ground. The velocity of the swing being high, before I could manage to make it stand still and before he could move, he was hurt in the scalp. Disembarking from the swing, I saw him braving all the hurt. Putting my palm on his head, the warmth of the blood oozing was palpable against the backdrop of cool water sprinkles of the rain. Something stirred in the heart centre of the little girl that I was, feeling guilty about the whole endeavour, but Debashish was unperturbed. Supporting and covering the scalp wound with a palm, rain soaked the two of us reached the dispensary to get the doctor uncle to bandage the wound. The wound was bandaged after cleansing and sacrificing some hair around it. The bandage was supported by tying across the lower jaw. We got our toffees from doctor uncle and reached back home, myself feeling apprehensive about the reaction of his parents. One remarkable feeling still indelible in my memory is complete absence of fear about the wound. Was I destined to be a medical professional?

Debashish's parents were very cool about all that had happened, taking it as a one of the usual occurrences in any child's life. The rest is history. With Dr. Verma uncle's wish to see me after almost ten years was an unwinding of pleasant innocent childhood days. More than four decades after, Debashish and I have no contact. Psychologically, I would like it to be this way, not knowing what life has made of that bright eyed, brilliant little fellow! I would rather cherish the memory.

# Case 3

# NCC Camp, Deolali

The Medical NCC unit had a fortnight's camp in summer as that was the time slot available from our curriculum with a regular final examination in October-November. Our annual camp was in the scenic cantonment of Deolali that year. There was no gender bar, and boys and girls were in the same camp in separate barracks. Deolali is a hill station. It was the month of hot summer, May. When our contingent left home the temp was about 44-45°C. We reached the campsite and were enchanted by its sheer picturesque delight. The weather was soothing, great relief from the scorching heat back home.

Away from bustling city life, nestling in the lap of nature, in a scenic valley necklaced by hills, our enthusiasm knew no bounds. Surrounding the parade ground outside the barracks was a cement tiled route, sizeable enough to accommodate a camp bed. Sleeping under the blue sky takes one back to "Night Among the Pines" of Stevenson. You are in a dreamland of fantasy in no time. Well, our age was tender, we were teenagers. We spread our camp beds on the tiled pavement in a series and very soon must have been fast asleep till we were woken up by a very cool breeze. It must have been just past midnight. Following natural instinct, each one tried to curl up to the foetal position, but soon the cool breeze was too cool. One by one we all got up, with sleep drooping eyelids, bundled up our bedding and rushed into the barracks for a cosy sleep. All of sudden, someone screamed with agony. This was Bibi. In the hustle-bustle and hurry her foot got entangled in the bed sheet and she struggled with the situation, one toenail was hurt by the sharp edge of a cement tile. The nail was partly avulsed. Again, a first encounter with a seemingly small trauma but excruciatingly painful in manifestation. Immediate and urgent medical care was given, but the night was terrible. The wound cooled and the bandage as well as some sheets got soaked with the blood and serum. Bibi's agony was on her face, stark and clear. I was reminded of Ann Frank's Diary where glimpses of Nazi torture camps are mentioned. This was an accident; what would happen if it was purposeful for the sake of torture was simply impossible to imagine. For Bibi, the fortnight of camp was like a nightmare with no parade, drill, only idling with a painful foot, sitting and watching the rest of us fit and fine, exercising and enjoying.

However, Bibi did not become a spoilsport, kept her good humour intact and joyfully participated in activities she could do with her traumatized great toe. The camp period was over soon and we reached back home for the rest of our summer vacation. The college reopened in due course and we were busy with our studies. Bibi's new nail was on our constant observation and practically we learnt about one of nature's miracles, its beautiful maneuvering and manipulating of one of the hardest tissues of the body. Bibi's new infant nail gradually gained strength and hardness and in a few months was just like its twin nail of the opposite great toe. True, Nature is the only Healer!

## Case 4

# An Unwarranted Emergency

Our NCC camp was in the scenic mountains of Deolali cantonment in Maharashtra. The sunset was approaching and we were preparing for the fall in for 6 o'clock attendance. Shikha came limping with one piece of footwear in hand. A giant thorn had pierced her right great toe and it hurt. I had considered myself an expert in removing thorns from the feet of friends irrespective of the situation. As Shikha was a case of thorn prick, I was ready. We sat down on two sizeable stones and I pulled the giant thorn from the flesh. Emergency ensued, profuse bleeding from the wound followed. It was just unstoppable in spite of our constant pressure. This was an unforeseen situation. We rushed to the MI room and got the wound dressed. However, even at night the bandage was fully soaked in blood.

This was a practical training for life time. A penetrating wound with any pointed weapon or object of other type has to be treated with due preparation. The pointed object in the body should not be suddenly removed as it plays the role of cork snugly fitting in the tissue. Sudden pulling out may result in incessant bleeding which for a grievous injury may prove fatal. This experience in the very first year of entering MBBS curriculum stood one in great stead throughout a professional career on emergency casualty duties. Life and its happenings are the greatest and the best educators.

# Case 5

# A Brave Mother

First childbirth is a psychological rebirth for married women or any woman who becomes a mother. Physiologically and psychologically the person changes. Rama got married relatively young. She was nineteen. Till then, she was a bright youngster, a friend living in the same colony. She was the youngest of the Banerjee siblings. After her marriage, Rama left the town to return after more than two years with a healthy baby. We were students in medical college then and life was our concern. Obstetrics was elusive to us as till then we had not practically seen any case of childbirth, the labour pains and its aftermath.

Thus Rama was for our young vision, a wonder; a senior with more life experience. And when she narrated her bravery in the labour room we were thrilled and also exulted. The labour table is specifically made so that the nurse or the doctor can sit at the foot end and help out the patient in labour. The labour wards are perpetually busy throughout 24 hrs, a day night cycle. Rama's experience of childbirth was unique. She was in labour on one table and there were other cases on other tables, separated by curtains. The nurse had gone to attend another case when Rama's baby came out. The brave young woman got up and with her own hands held her newborn steadily till the nurse returned. What a presence of mind! And here was Rama with her wonderful baby, the unique one who arrived in his mother's palms.

# Case 6

# Miss Khare

Three messages reached me in a span of three days that one of my schoolteachers was admitted in the Radiotherapy ward for radiation therapy. Entry to Radiotherapy units is a little stringent and time schedule is strictly observed. Due to pressure of clinical work and teaching I could visit Miss Khare, our chemistry teacher in school after two days of receiving the first message. From the entrance I saw two affectionate eyes with a weak body, distended abdomen and pale face. It appeared as though she was waiting for me. As I went near, she smiled, did not talk anything about her disease, pain or discomfort but blessed me from her heart. She said she was very proud of me and wished I should remember to work for the needy without greed ever creeping in my psyche. This was a surprise. Never had she been so personal in expression of ideas and ideology. Glimpses of her Spartan life, floated in my vision. She lived in a small house, all by herself. She was unmarried and had a poor young relative who studied and looked after her. As a chemistry teacher, she was excellent and teaching was more than a profession for her, it was a vocation.

As I left the ward that day with a promise to visit her, hardly did I realize the scene would change completely. Next day, the staff nurse said the patient expired just about an hour after my visit. It dawned upon me that she was waiting for me to say those few words. Most humbly, I have tried to live up to my teacher's ideals and expectations till date.

# Case 7

# Mapari and Lal

Our medical college has provision for 200 new admissions to MBBS course every year. We were also admitted with our 200 strong batch of students. Life style changes drastically on entry to medical college. The curriculum is very demanding on your time, hard work and intelligence. We become more and more focussed as we pass from event to event. There is little scope and margin for admitting untoward life events. But life's map is not charted by us anyway. We came to know that one of our classmates, Mapari, was very ill. He had developed deep jaundice (viral hepatitis) and was admitted to the infectious diseases ward with coma. As students of first year (pre-clinical) we had not visited infectious diseases wards which were in another campus not very far off. In a large group we went to visit him. He was in one of the side rooms. He was comatose and was visibly looking yellow though his complexion was dark. This was the first encounter with a comatose patient for most of us, and he was our classmate. Within a few days, Mapari succumbed to his life threatening disease.

A few years later another student, Lal, who was a Nepali died in hepatic coma and there was rumour that every year one student died from a new batch of 200 admissions. We did not have the courage to look into the statistics of such a sad happening, but I got interested in the subject, infectious diseases and hepatitis which is with me even now, with one conviction, that acute diseases (infectious diseases) should be curable totally with judicious and timely treatment. In Medicine most of the ailments are only managed, very few can be totally cured, infectious diseases are such.

# Case 8

# A Case of Smallpox

Smallpox (Variola) was a dreadful disease which challenged the medical world for centuries. The first vaccination with cowpox vaccine was experimented with by none other than the Father of Immunology Edward Jenner in the last decade of the eighteenth century. Against the backdrop of devil's dance by smallpox in epidemic proportion with most surviving adults having pockmarked disfigured faces sometimes with blindness due to corneal opacities, the smooth complexion of a milkmaid drew his scientific attention. The secret of her smooth and flawless skin was her tryst with cowpox. The medical scientist got a clue which would lead to a great boon for humanity. His experiments of making cowpox vaccine and administering this to human volunteers must have been an uphill task at a time when scientific medical knowledge in the west was in its infancy. Two centuries later, WHO declared the planet free of smallpox in 1980. The last batch of infants vaccinated for smallpox was those born in 1980.

Prior to 1980, there were hoardings by WHO for awarding any person finding a case of smallpox. We had never seen a case of smallpox but only adults with pockmarked faces and some rare one-eyed beggars, resulting from corneal opacity by smallpox virus infection. The first and the only case of smallpox that I saw was in the early seventies. Such news spreads like wildfire in a medical college campus. The case was in the Infectious Diseases Wards in our hospital. She was a tribal woman in her forties, kept in an isolated room. The sight of the patient was very pathetic; skin, the largest sense organ of our body with its function of protection to internal tissues, temperature regulation and immunological functions was devastated in this patient. The pustules of smallpox covered almost 80% of her skin. She had bilateral corneal lesions also. Her agony was unbearable even to the onlookers. She succumbed within a few days. The debt of mankind to the father of vaccination practically became clear like blue sky. We owe our immunity from smallpox to Jenner.

Man learns from history that he learns not history. Natural smallpox could be wiped out from the globe, but in some secret defense laboratories the smallpox virus is stored for biological warfare. Creation takes so much time of decades and even centuries, destruction could be very fast. May the Almighty, bestow goodwill to Man of intellect to use his talents in the right direction.

# Case 9

# Rabies in a Case Mauled by Tiger

Rabies is called Hydrophoebia, wherein the sufferer has excessive salivation and intense pharyngeal muscle spasm whenever trying to gulp water. The face has a persistent look of apprehension. This is a viral disease affecting the nervous system with severe and irreversible complications leading to fatality. The death is very tragic, some may become completely paralysed, others very violent, even wanting to bite any onlooker. It is infectious spreading by body secretions, though there are no case reports of human bite causing rabies. Animals of many species like canines and rodents are the carriers of the virus. The case fatality rate being one hundred percent, it is very dreadful. Immunization is available for persons exposed to situations warranting a chance of contracting the infection but not suffering from rabies clinically.

This patient was an Adivasi women, robust in build who was mauled by a tiger during her sojourn in the woods for search of domestic fuel. She was in a terrible state with her muscle deep wounds which were raw and very painful. Any wound suspected to have been contaminated by rabies virus is kept open for natural sterilization. The agony of the patient still haunts in my memory stores. Intense and persistent pharyngeal muscle spasms causing inability to gulp even a sip of water, she was just in a pathetic condition. She also had spasms with air and so the ceiling fan was off in the month of April, which is quite hot in our town.

Medical doctors are keepers of health and life. Rare is a time when one wishes release of the soul of a case with intense agony, specially in cases of severe burns, terminal diseases with intractable pain or a case like severe rabies with excruciating muscle spasms and pain. We are just silent spectators confronting rabies cases. No treatment works, death is the only escape. Finally she was quiet after severe spasms and lay on her hospital bed, dead. The pathos etched on the face of her ignorant labourer husband is indescribable.

I remember a prayer in my school hymn book.

"Count your blessings, name them one by one and it will surprise you what the lord has done."

Man's unending quest for more wealth, fortune, fame makes him forget the sheer joy of living a healthful life, until calamity strikes. Caring for patients as a physician is a very demanding job, their joys and sorrows engulf us, may even overwhelm or may cause apathy. The childhood habit of counting blessings and thanking the Supreme for a Brand New Day every dawn has been my constant energy source. Life is beautiful as such without any tag when one is fresh in mind, healthy in body and cheerful in spirit.

# Case 10

## The Lady in White

Krishnamurthy auntie was operated for a tumour. This was a major surgery, so she would be resting for ten days in hospital, and then gradually bounce back to full activity three months after discharge from hospital. I visited her after surgery in the ward side room. As I reached the vicinity of the room there was immense peace. It was rising like an island from the sea of chaos in the general ward.

Auntie was resting and her face was calm. The room, a normal hospital ward side room, seemed illumined by light of the 'lady in white.' By auntie's bedside stood she, the lady in white. Her attire was a simple, khadi white saree with a narrow border and a white khadi blouse. She was fair, but in reality her complexion was shining with her inner light. She wore glasses and her thick hair was put in a plait. This was a unique experience, indelible in memory, a finite form and infinite beauty. Till then I had never seen or met an individual with so much ethereal light. I was not even initiated to anything like spirituality at that age of just twenty years. This lady was auntie's youngest sister. She, I later learnt, was highly educated, left her job of lecturer to join 'Belur Math,' sister concern of 'Ramkrishna Mission.'

Because of her reputation as a good amateur nurse she was called upon to be by the bedside of her sister. After more than three decades, my conviction has remained unshaken that 'chhoti mousi' (younger aunt) is the most beautiful woman I have seen in my life. That day my young mind was convinced that nursing is much more important than doctoring. One needs to be patient, peaceful and humble to serve others. A picture perfect was she, the living spirit of Florence Nightingale 'the lady with the lamp.' To be able to serve with patience and peace is real service. The lady in white is my inspiration in patient care.

God does not live in Heaven alone. He walks with us in everyday life, in the form of living infiniteness, although visible in rare individuals.

# Case 11

# For Love

A new batch of registered students for M.D. come to the department every year. Over a month's time we get to know them through work, emergency duties and postgraduate classes. Vaibhav was in that batch and his surname struck a chord of memory. Was he one of our past teacher's relatives? The answer was in the affirmative. He was his son. His father, who was in the department, had died due to chronic poisoning. For about a month before his final departure from our mortal world he had consumed a bit of poison everyday as a chronic suicidal attempt. The question was why? Nuclear Medicine was gaining ground and a small nuclear medicine laboratory was set up by the department. This lecturer was in-charge of that laboratory. Radioisotope was indented from Bhabha Atomic Research Commission and it had duly arrived. The purpose was to use it for diagnostics. In a casual way, he took the container with isotope home and put it in his refrigerator. Incidentally, his wife was diagnosed with a case of acute leukaemia (blood cancer) to which she succumbed. The young doctor could not forgive himself for his negligence and so planned his sacrifice. He started consuming poison daily and after one month left for another world, leaving their two year old son to the care of grandparents.

The incidents took place when we were undergraduate students and Vaibhav, their child, now a young man in his mid twenties was with us as postgraduate student. It seemed like a full circle. At the time of the young doctor committing suicide to punish himself for his wife's leukaemia, there was gossip everywhere as to the wisdom in this action. Firstly, though none should be negligent in handling of radioisotopes, however, that as the trigger for his wife's leukaemia was only conjectural. Secondly, had the event been reversed and a man died young, the wife, the mother of the child or children lives to bring them up. Human dutifulness is undefined, without limits or boundaries. They are individualized. The question which comes to mind is to whom are we answerable for our duties? The young doctor sacrificed his life for love for his wife but probably could not do justice to the bud of their conjugal love, their only son.

# Case 12

## Unfulfilled Ambition

Dr. Sunitee Roy, a medical graduate from Kolkata, was doing M.D. (Obstetrics and Gynaecology) in our medical college. She had come to the state of Maharashtra because of her husband's posting. By dint of hard work and persuasive efforts with the university she secured a berth for M.D. in the subject. This was before the entrance tests for P.G. admissions began. She was quiet, sincere and studious. Everything was fine till a day when Sunitee discovered that she was getting fever for some days. Like most doctors, she brushed it aside, taking occasional paracetamol. Gradually, fever took the upper hand, the doctor felt some discomfort in one of the thigh regions with throbbing pain off and on. All this time her driving force was her examinations which were due in a month's time. Medical curriculum is heavy and perseverance and hard work are essential. She did not want to take any chances and hence the neglect of her health.

However, the disease marched with destiny in the reverse direction and one day she was admitted with a deep abscess. The abscess was drained, antibiotics and supportive treatment was started. Day after day, her condition worsened as the abscess burst in the rectum followed by septicemia. A pregnant woman (she was pregnant) is often more susceptible to complications due to physiological alterations in the body. Septicemia caused her to be delirious sometimes and during such spans, Sunitee only had one wish, to write her M. D exams. She muttered she would have to study again all these voluminous books in her next birth because to get an M.D. degree was her only ambition. She wanted to live to fulfil her ambition. It was a pathetic scenario. Scientific knowledge, medical and nursing care and prayers of friends and relatives were beaten by death. The ambition remained unfulfilled.

In Ayurveda, it is documented that there are one hundred and one ways of death and of these only one is the actual & real, which is inevitable, the other hundred are possible but avoidable or treatable with timely treatment. In Sunitee's case the avoidable one was probably converted to the unavoidable due to her neglect and delay in taking treatment.

# Case 13

## Dr. Leena Dey

Dr. Leena Dey was an ideal medical teacher for us. We all aspired to be like her. She personified every attribute our young minds could think of. She was master of her subject, an excellent teacher for bedside clinics as well as lectures. She presented clinical cases in clinical meetings most scientifically, with very good language. Dr. Dey had an inherent smartness and grace in her. Academically she was very bright, intelligent and humane towards patient care, simple yet knowledgeable in her way of teaching. She was our ideal. She married another physician and, thereafter, changed her discipline. She became a gynaecologist. With two M.D. degrees, in Internal Medicine and Obstetrics and Gynaecology, she was an exception par excellence, Research was in her blood and she excelled in this field also.

Two decades passed, slowly a disease crept in. She was diagnosed as a case of cancer, was operated upon and subsequently was on medication. Undaunted, madam continued with teaching, patient care, academic and administrative duties and research. Cancer was defeated prima facie but surfaced after a few years. Dr. Leena Dey developed secondary metastasis and paralysis of the legs. She was bedridden but books and the Internet were her dearest companions. She kept abreast of newer advances, discussed medical issues with visitors and callers. Her scientific spirit was unmatched. There are so many men of science around, rare is the individual with genuine scientific spirit, and Leena Dey was that rare gem.

Relentlessly, persistently, the disease progressed, the physical body died but not the ethereal. As a spirit of science, medicine, intellectual, honest academics and excellent research, she is immortal in our memory.

# Part II

## Widening Horizons

*Sometimes people are beautiful.*
*Not in looks,*
*Not in what they say,*
*Just in what they are.*

*—Markus Zusak*

# Case 1

# Urmila

An adolescent girl, fourteen years in age was admitted to surgical ward. She had a tumour near the knee on one side. There was no pain and the rate of growth was significant hence investigations were undertaken. The x-ray told the untold story and it was a malignant growth, a fast growing cancer of bone osteosarcoma. Multilating surgery with amputation above the knee was the option. The person, Urmila was full of inherent beauty. She had a pleasant voice and could hold audience with her storytelling capacity. A student of grade eight or nine, she was just above average in her class. The real beauty was her zest for life complimented by a pair of eloquent eyes. The parents as well as the patient herself were gradually and convincingly motivated about the essentiality of the mutilating surgery. This is one Waterloo for doctors, especially when external organ removal is concerned. Internal maneuvers with physiological alterations are somewhat less difficult because man's vision is bound by external form and morphometry.

The medical students talked to Urmila with some apprehension about psychological state for the said amputation. Undeterred was her spirit. She laughed and joked as usual. Somewhere, I had doubt if she had registered the happening or not. I was wrong. After surgery, Urmila was her usual self, her lively spirit undaunted, her zest of life soaring high. The movie "Anand" was running in theatres then. She said she admired Anand's spirit to live and live with joy. She was a walky talky Anand to us. In due course of days, she was discharged with other therapeutic advices. A few weeks passed and three months. Urmila came with crutches with the same spirit. She could not go to school so studied at home to write her final examination of the academic year. Destiny had another option for her. Within six months Urmila had a recurrence in the other leg and amputation followed. Now she was dependent physically and sat in her bed with support to her back. Her spirit was invincible for her disease.

Then, there was the final fatal blow. News spread like wildfire in the student community that Urmila was admitted with multiple metastases in the lungs and was probably at the brink of mortality. With burdened heart, we visited her. She was breathless, and looked physically debilitated. With a smile on her lips and twinkle in her eyes this courageous girl said, "Please don't feel sorry, you know Anand always lives and never dies. I will also live with you all."

Yes, and Urmila still lives with me after more than three decades as an immortal being. My question then and now is only one, "Is there death?"

# Case 2

# Pramod

"Doctor, will you marry me?" was the question Pramod asked the lady physician of that ward. He must have been almost her age, in his early twenties. The house physician was more knowledgeable about the condition of her patient. She was unable to convince him about doctor-patient relation, a critical and delicate issue. A doctor's concern and care may be mistaken for personal emotional involvement. The art of medical practice to be compassionate with empathy with a neutral attitude in respect of the emotional side especially with gender difference is challenging. The smart, efficient and dutiful young house physician had a human problem staring at her directly. Pramod was the only son of widow. Tragically, he had bilateral polycystic disease of the kidneys and was in renal failure.  In kidney failure, encephalopathy sets in and behaviour and neurological functions get altered.

Pramod's lifespan was now in known finite time. The only difference between a normal healthy person and a dying patient is perhaps the finiteness of the end in terms of time. Pramod's case was such. He saw his mother in her white saree and had premonitions about his life's end. He confided in his mother that this doctor was his love. She, in his eyes, was the epitome of every virtue that he dreamt of and if she could bear his child, the mother would not be left lonely. Intelligently, the mother confided in the senior doctor and requested him to change the duty of the lady doctor if possible. The senior physician fathomed the situation and arranged the duties.

Pramod continued to be delirious and pleaded and cried for a glimpse of his love interest. The situation was emotionally charged. The mother could not afford a side room with payment, but his delirious talk became a nuisance for other patients. The wise and humane senior physician overruled every rule and shifted him to the side room. He was becoming bad to worse. The mother could not afford any expensive treatment options and Pramod, with his genetically inherited bilateral polycystic kidneys, was doomed with his destiny. The end came.

A few months later, the mother came to meet the house physician. Holding the doctor's hands she asked her forgiveness for all her son said. What a courageous, and broad minded woman she was. They talked for a while. The lady had accepted her fate and worked for a charitable organization to help physically challenged children. Life came full circle. Pramod's wish was fulfilled and his mother was not lonely. The young house physician learnt her first lesson in the most critical of human emotions, love and empathy in medical practice.

## Case 3

# Motghare

One of those very busy admission days it was with more than thirty new cases by evening with twelve more hours before 6 a.m. next morning, the time scheduled for the following OPD and another emergency unit. As a routine in Medical Colleges, admission days run by rotation with one unit working on a particular day for every clinical department. The house-physicians have to work with case histories of newly admitted patients, attend to immediate emergency care and finish a few routine laboratory investigations like urine examination, haemoglobin and blood counts for the chief's grand rounds next morning (ward side labs are not functional now).

The interns and the house-physician had worked incessantly from 7.30 a.m to 6 p.m. that Tuesday, of the thirty odd new cases, more than half were with fever of various durations. Cases with pyrexia are intriguing for the resident doctors as lot of investigations may be necessary serially depending upon response to therapy or results of history, examination and investigations already done. The workout for each case is different and can be sometimes very trying.

On that Tuesday, all slides were prepared and kept ready for scrutiny at the earliest available time slot. One patient on bed 11 was a young man, Motghare. He was arrogant and uncooperative, opposing every endeavour of the resident doctor. He even refused to lie down for examination. He was one of those cases admitted with fever. Late that night, the resident physician scrutinized the blood smear slide and to her dismay Motghare's peripheral blood smear slide was suggestive of highly increased white blood cells, a probable diagnosis of blood cancer, leukaemia. She got a jolt and decided to take one more smear to be surer. The patient was approached for the pinprick next morning and as in the evening before, he vehemently reacted with a negative answer.

In the chief's grand rounds, all cases were discussed and later, he visited the ward side laboratory to see important slides. He saw Motghare's slide and agreed with the resident doctor's diagnosis. The arrogant reluctance of the patient was reported, hence he personally requested Motghare to cooperate. The patient condescended. However, this was only the initial event as with diagnosis of leukaemia, he would need many pricks almost every day. With his clinical experience and deep perception of human behaviour, he guessed what lay ahead. While leaving after clinical work that day he called the house-physician and said "I know he is arrogant and is going to misbehave, but he has leukaemia. Try and see if you can pardon him for that."

Bedside manners are routinely taught in medical curriculum, but the patients have no such training. It sometimes gets difficult to deal with vagaries of human nature. In this particular case the house physician took up the challenge and Motghare received his treatment, though not for too long a period. I am perplexed at the bilateral happening observed over my clinical experience, patients have behavioural problems, is that cause or the effect of physical ailments. They are interlinked for sure.

# Case 4

# Padmakar

Thirty nine year old lean and slim Padmakar reported to the emergency unit after discomfort in his chest. He was out on a tour. There was a strong family history of ischaemic heart disease, the patient himself was apparently without modifiable risk factors like lifestyle, tobacco intake, high blood pressure, diabetes. He was a quiet man. His wife was a picture of anxiety, apprehension, and fear, all drawn on her countenance. The electrocardiogram showed inferior myocardial infarction. Immediate angiography was not in vogue then and the facility was not accessible in our city.

With conservative management he improved well and was duly discharged. He was advised the usual period of rest. Regular follow up was done and it was smooth sailing except for his wife's perpetual anxiety ridden face. She would follow him like a shadow. Once she fainted while viewing an informative medical episode about heart attack on television. The situation was paradoxical. The patient was improving, but the young wife was at risk of becoming neurotic. Padmakar joined his office and was his usual self, silent, peaceful. He and his cardiogram fully recovered. He was a very obedient and disciplined patient. Two years later he was detected to be mildly diabetic and he is on oral therapy till date.

At the age of seventy he is without any cardiac problem at all with strong genetic predisposition. The family history was very bad. Parents and all eight siblings had heart disease and diabetes. In spite of such genetic background Padmakar is peacefully continuing retired life. Can genetics be modified by mental attitude, discipline and faith? In Padmakar's case that seems to have happened.

# Case 5

# Asha

One postgraduate student asked a junior lecturer of Medicine about a case. His foster sister Asha was probably suffering from some type of kidney disease. This junior lecturer, a fresh M.D. was a bit surprised that the P.G. put so much trust in her. Asha was in her late twenties, married for more than a decade with no children. She was shy, reticent and scared of social taboo for being childless. This made her rather unwilling to see a physician for her symptoms of swelling over the face and feet off and on. She attributed most of the urinary symptoms to her inability to conceive. As this young lecturer was a lady, so the PG could persuade Asha to visit medical college OPD. Asha was a bundle of nerves denying all queries, brushing aside all possibilities of any disease. Examination revealed that she was a case of nephritis, an inflammation of the kidneys, the cause of which is variable. Apart from routine investigations, special investigations for kidney disease, a biopsy was essential.

From details of her history, it was obvious that the reason for infertility was with her spouse. This fact emboldened the lecturer to persuade her to accept the procedure of biopsy for proper diagnosis. Asha was apprised of her neutrality towards the marital problem of childlessness. So a biopsy was done. The report spelt doom in the near future. With membranoproliferative glomerulonephritis Asha could live for five to six years. All modalities of available treatments were tried but benefits were short-lived. We were at the wrong end of our endeavour. Just about that time we came across a book on auto-urine therapy. After brain teasing discussions we decided to convince her to try this. In the meanwhile, a young lady came to Asha with her proposal of donating a kidney to her, which was turned down by her vehemently.

Auto urine therapy was started after all formalities of investigations were completed. Asha showed gradual and persistent improvement in her health status. We also considered psychological rehabilitation. She was sent for D. Ed and Montessari training against the backdrop of strong opposition from her in-law's family. The husband accepted it and encouraged her. Bright as she was, she came out of the examinations in flying colours, got a job as a teacher in a school. A new Asha emerged like a phoenix. Gone was the timid, shy, inhibited being and a bright, cheerful, progressive woman was born. She is a very good teacher till date at the age of sixty years.

There are no diseases, only sick persons. A diagnosis which spelt doom for the patient in less than a decade's time could not survive against human effort and will. Asha is very much alive, without any treatment and/or complications pertaining to her kidney disease.

# Case 6

# Scleroderma

Scleroderma is an autoimmune disease. It affects the skin which becomes smooth and shiny. The fingertips become tapering and gradually shrink in dimension. The face looks pinched with cheeks hollowed, eyelids blink less and the hair of eyebrows and eyelashes becomes sparse. They may get other complications like difficulty in swallowing, telengiectasia, calcinosis etc. Meherbanu was about forty years of age when she was diagnosed as a case of scleroderma. She sat on her bed observing every activity of the ward with keen interest. The house physician had a beautiful rapport with this patient.

In her spare time, she asked Meherbanu who called her "Memsahab" about her family. The family was well-off financially. Her sons were studying. She had one daughter. The doctor asked her if she would educate her daughter. Back came the reply, she would not mind if that girl could be bright and dedicated like this young lady house physician. The doctor was in dismay as to what made this illiterate patient think that she was bright or intelligent. She pondered and that night realised that communications exist without words and gestures. This realisation was unique. Meherbanu died due to progress of her disease, but the little wisdom she passed on to the young doctor made her wiser towards understanding fellow human beings with silent communication, beyond use of words.

## Case 7

# A Case of AIDS with Tuberculosis

In the early eighties, HIV-AIDS was in an initial phase of enquiry and discussions in medical academic circles. The first cases were those with homosexual behaviour reported from a geographic pocket in the USA in 1981. For us, in India the issue was more conjectural than real. Most of us then were naïve enough to trust social behaviour of our countrymen to be straightforward. Promiscuity we imagined was uncommon. We also had the notion that homosexuality was even rare in occurrence except in special groups like prison inmates, police and army barracks and the like. Intravenous drug users were not common either. Most of us had not seen any case of HIV-AIDS.

News about unusual cases spreads like wildfire in the medical college campus because a large fraternity of students, resident doctors and teachers devour knowledge and experience of clinical cases. We learnt there was a patient in the tuberculosis ward with some features of HIV-AIDS with diagnosis established by laboratory tests. Curiosity drove us to the patient. We were aware that our behaviour must be such as not to cause embarrassment or anxiety in a patient already burdened by his pain and sorrow.

The poor, emaciated man was sitting on his bed with blank eyes fixed at an unknown point in space. He was expressionless, though without any physical distress. Vital functions were stable. Gradually, methodically, very cautiously we went into the clinical history, behavioural history, family history. He replied with the same blank expression. He was in his early thirties, a labourer, married with two little children. His wife was also a daily wage labourer. He plainly accepted having the usual extramarital encounters with commercial workers without any tinge of guilt or remorse.

This rural, less civilized, illiterate man was not just aware of social taboo about extramarital relations. So there was no stigma attached. We coaxed him to find out if he knew about his disease. He admitted that he has some disease for which he needs regular and long term treatment. That was all! It took me a few days to realise the extent of ignorance in which he lives with many like him. This was in 1986. Nightmares haunted me to even imagine what giant shape would replace stray cases of the HIV-AIDS phenomenon. Twenty years later, the probability had become a gigantic truth when most medicine wards in Mumbai J.J. Hospital were teaming with full-blown cases of morbid HIV-AIDS cases with multiple and varied infections!

# Case 8

# An Enigmatic Case

The man had fierce eyes, the abdomen was distended and he was unkempt. There were a few queer looking individuals around him. They said he was their master. What kind of master could this man be, so shabby, almost dirty in his bearing? The folks around him were reluctant to tell us about any details of this master's lifestyle, family etc. The scenario was difficult to fathom, intriguing. Maybe some cult practitioner of sorts. Due to foul odour from his body he was put on a bed in the verandah of the ward. Routine practice in medical rounds of teaching hospitals is to discuss the cases from an academic viewpoint. This case was also discussed in detail with probable differential diagnosis. One possibility was HIV-AIDS. This was 1985, HIV-AIDS was not a fashionable diagnosis in India then. The proverb, walls have ears was practically substantiated. Next day, there was front page news in a local daily newspaper with a question as to whether the first case of HIV-AIDS was diagnosed in a government medical college hospital.

All our unit doctors were summoned by the Dean for inquiry. Persons in authority have their peculiar behavioural patterns, one such trait is to overwhelm their subordinates to extract some statement in their favour out of fear. We were to face unknown charges that day. All are learning experiences in life's journey. So was this one. One committee member asked about the modus operandi of the news leaking to the press. We were indeed innocent. They disbelieved us. Then they asked how it reached the press. Well, in a democratic country speech is free and interpretation of what is heard depends upon the receiver. What he will do with the information can neither be predicted nor interfered with. The chief of the committee was visibly angry at our naivette. The meeting ended with a warning to us against taking the help of the media. Truth was on our side so we were fearless.

A few weeks later, a second meeting was called and we were told that serology for HIV-AIDS was negative. My reaction as the head of the unit was that, the report could be true or cooked not to give credit of being 'numero uno' in this diagnosis. Skepticism of this type afflicts many authorities. They have discrimination and their own way of determinism about institutions under their supervision. Alas! Only if they realised that, longevity of institutions is far more than that of individuals. Knowledge is light and to dispel darkness needs to be accepted with openness.

## Case 9

# A Case of Drowning

The young patient occupied a bed near the door of the ward. In general ward such a bed is a privileged one because the patient is under constant observation. The flip side of the position of the bed is disturbance by passers through the door. This case was a case of drowning in a deep well from where he was rescued and after immediate help was brought to medical college. In the critical period after admission he needed tracheostomy making passage in the trachea for ventilation of the lungs, which then healed completely. The only problem of the patient was lack of speech. He was otherwise ambulant and could comprehend usual situations around him.

Accidental drowning has various consequences, depending on the trauma received to the head and other parts of the body, the asphyxia period after being rescued and complications with infection setting in especially in the respiratory system.

I must have observed this case for about a month and a half in the same condition. We made sure that his speech was really involved and that he was not feigning. A big surprise was in store for us when one fine day, my house physician reported that he was able to speak, clearly without any disability whatsoever. He then confided that till then, he was persistently making efforts to speak. His efforts were duly rewarded by fate. He went home with a lease of life. Young as he was, he could not describe the incident of his rendezvous with the near death situation.

# Case 10

## The Last Supper

In Medicine wards, we took evening rounds between 6 and 8 p.m. This also coincided with supper time for the indoor patients. The coincidence was because as house-physicians we could directly see patients being served proper and prescribed hospital diet, whether they ate well or not. I enjoyed this time because the house-physician was all alone, the only doctor available. The time was educative for knowing the patients' reactions to routine activities like eating supper, washing hands and so on.

That young patient was a teenager, with dark complexion and a handsome face. He had multiple heart valve problems, was from a very poor family. He went in and out of medical wards frequently. He was often a case for medical examinations. He was so knowledgeable about his medical examination that often he reminded the student of some point had he missed that. We all knew him well and he was a family member of our ward. With chronic heart failure there were restrictions about his diet. That evening, the food was a bit unusual as there was a sweet (besan laddoo) with 'puris' (fried home made bread), with restriction of salt, the diet must be unpalatable and monotonous. That, evening he gestured me to come and sought permission to eat normal food. There was a compelling appeal in his shining eyes. He promised sincere obedience in future without asking for undue favours. His only wish was to have a normal plate of food that evening.

I accepted. He was served the normal plate of food, which would be put on his cardiac table (a stool, for person to bend forward). The unalloyed joy and satisfaction on his face when he was served a normal plate is unforgettable. There was no greed for food in his expression, simply immense satisfaction. He was in bed no. 2. I asked him to eat and moved to see the other patients. On turning back towards this boy after a few minutes, I found him sitting still, with a faint smile on his countenance and a half eaten sweet in his right hand.

The last supper remained unfinished. Elders say if a sick person wishes to eat something special, it is best to serve it, so that desire is fulfilled. This was a practical proof. Though our Krishna could not eat his last supper, his soul was satisfied and left his body without suffering.

# Case 11

# A Case of Renal Failure

The patient was in the side room of the ward. He was a case of chronic renal failure on dialysis regularly. He was in his mid forties and his wife in her early forties was always by his bedside, tending to every need of the patient. This lady was too intelligent, unusual in a way. She had large eyes, was bespectacled and slim. Whenever, there was the chance she discussed medical matters about kidney failure and keenly observed all activities of the ward whenever she could.

One day, we discovered lot of sweet lemons on the side cupboard by the patient's bedside. With high potassium content too many fruits, especially citrus ones is not advisable for kidney patients. This was duly conveyed to her. A few days later the same instance was repeated followed by our instructions. Life in the ward and of this patient continued. The wife was trying to take the patient for transplantation as and when possible and feasible.

On one evening round, the house physician said the renal failure patient died that afternoon. Undoubtedly, death can come to anyone at any time, but medical men need to know and understand the immediate acute cause as well as circumstances for the occurrence. He said he was summoned from his quarters by an urgent call from the ward. He rushed to find that the patient's heart had stopped, arranged for immediate electrocardiogram and withdrawal of sample of blood. The cardiogram showed evidence of hyperkalemia (rise in serum levels of potassium). He instituted treatment before the biochemistry report came but to no avail. The patient succumbed. The biochemistry report arrived in due time with the laboratory technician rushing with the report as he sensed the emergency. The serum potassium levels were more than double the maximum normal limits for the laboratory.

Like a flash the sweet lemons floated in front of my eyes. The wife had continued to feed him fruits in spite of repeated instructions, she said in good faith that fruits are good for sick persons. This woman was more than average in intelligence. It is a million dollar question worth pondering as to whether she fed those fruits in good faith, with stubborn, doggedness or it was on purpose to see what happens. Alas ! There was no time for double verification!

# Case 12

# Copper Sulphate Poisoning

She was in her early twenties, studying B.Sc with chemistry as one of her subjects. She belonged to lower middle class and was from a backward community. They lived in a suburb of the main city in a low cost dwelling. Most of her relatives were illiterate or just had primary education. She was good in studies so had reached B.Sc level. Science and scientists were subjects of keen interest to her. She had a passion for reading about lives of scientists, their struggles & risks they incurred for their scientific pursuits. This gradually became etched in her psyche. She wanted to be a scientist and wished even to become a Nobel Laureate some day. This far was very nice indeed.

With her overzealous scientific mind, experimentation she considered essential. In a chemistry laboratory there are many chemicals. She got fascinated by copper sulphate and read about the properties, reactions, tried a few as and when possible with varied results. To cap it all she desired to knew if this was really toxic for humans. She started consuming a small quantity of copper sulphate almost every day and came to medical college for kidney failure. The history of chemical intake did not occur to resident doctors immediately and the usual time of investigations continued. One day, I discovered a small bottle with the greenish blue powder on the side cupboard of her bed. This was a surprise. Out of curiosity I queried as to what it was and she said, "Well it is copper sulphate, which I am consuming to find out if that really causes kidney failure." Gosh! A thunderbolt! The reason of kidney failure was discovered. Inquisitiveness made me question her about what other chemicals she had tried to taste and the answer was shocking. She had consumed many in different quantities including mercury. Our heads were reeling at the mind of a budding scientist, with very little chance of blossoming.

# Case 13

# The Staff Nurse

She was breathless on admission, even at rest. Her heart rate was fast and irregular. She was having a dysrrhythmia of cardiac rhythm, atrial fibrillation. The treatment as well as investigations began. Auscultation of the heart revealed murmurs (abnormal sounds between the normal heart sounds). There are some characteristics by which murmurs are described in medical terminology. One such characteristic is change in intensity of sound of murmur with posture. With a very rapid heart rate, it is difficult to appreciate features of murmur, still her murmur was perceived to slightly change its quality on posture change. This is a specific indicator of a rare cause of heart valve problems, called left-atrial myxoma. Myxoma in simple terms can be put as a small fleshy mass attached to the inner surface of the heart muscle of one chamber, the left atrium. This mass may have a small stalk and based on that will be able to swing inside with the flow of blood. In this swing, it can block one of the valves often (in this case the valve between the left atrium and the left ventricle, the mitral valve). This can break into very small pieces, called emboli which can get dislodged in circulation and get lodged in the vascular system causing block in circulation of that part of the body.

So, with no other significant past history and changing intensity of the murmur with atrial fibrillation this woman (a staff nurse) in the medical college could be a rare case of left atrial myxoma. A rare case always draws lots of interested students like a magnet drawing the iron filings. Of course, comfort of the patient needs to be taken care of. The academic aspect is that if students do not see cases, how will they practically learn the science of medicine? The medical and nursing community get VIP treatment in medical college hospitals, quite naturally. They cannot be compelled to allow everyone to examine them like other patients. However, this lady was very cooperative and was intelligent enough to understand the value of such learning experiences for students. She accepted repeated auscultations by P.G. students graciously.

Investigations proved that the case was indeed of left atrial myxoma and she was to be operated upon with anticoagulants to prevent embolisation. A proper balance of dose of anticoagulants, timing and operative procedure is absolutely necessary. She was operated upon in a good cardiothoracic unit and returned hale and hearty after a few months. Timely diagnosis, efficient medical personnel and a relatively cooperative and rather healthful individual can get immense benefit from technology.

# Case 14

# Asphyxia

When one wishes to visit a sick person, one carries fruits as a token signifying good wishes. Can fruits be toxic in some cases? An elderly man was lying with many complaints pertaining to many systems of the body for investigations and treatment thereof. He was on a bed near one pillar in the ward. At about 4 p.m. one afternoon the staff nurse on duty was summoned to his bed by a student nurse who went to administer some medicines to the patient because she found the man gasping. She was aghast that someone who was just walking around was in such a state all of a sudden. The staff nurse rushed to the spot, tried to revive the patient. The ward boy came with the emergency tray, the house physician was urgently summoned telephonically. He rushed immediately. The anesthetist was called and after intubation a full grape was removed. However, with all efforts, which took its usual few minutes (fifteen to twenty) for all this happened in a routine case in a general ward, the patient could not be saved.

The mystery was solved on seeing the full, unchewed grape which the wife fed him after he returned from toilet in good faith to give him nourishment. The edentulous man could not control the rolling down of the smooth fruit from gullet to the trachea and was thus chocked to death by asphyxia. The wife realized her mistake, of course life had already departed from that frail old man's body by then.

# Case 15

## A Case of Peritoneal Dialysis

The major discipline of internal medicine encompasses many sub branches. In the last one and a half decades super specialties in these branches have become the in thing. Prior to that M.D. physicians acquired training in house or from abroad in a superspecialty and were permitted to start a superspecialty division under the main discipline. This incident belongs to that period of academic medical history. Our head of the department of internal medicine, who was an excellent physician, was also trained in Nephrology from abroad. Under his able guidance the Nephrology unit began to function for the first time in our part of the country. This was more than thirty years back. Patients of chronic renal failure are pathetic cases to be taken care of. They have very fluctuating metabolic parameters and are constantly in fluxes with respect to health and disease states. Protein and salt intake being restricted they could become cachexic. Calcium, iron supplements are required. Sometimes anemia becomes unresponsive and to stimulate red cell production erythropoietin is required. Due to multiple etiological factors they can bleed and need cautious blood transfusions. They usually have hypertension, retain salt and water excessively in the body and become bloated up. To cap it all they have immune disturbances and infections are a constant threat. Drug dosages need meticulous maneuvering because of metabolic chaos in the milieu.

This case was one of our first cases of peritoneal dialysis. Fluid exchange is done via the semipermeable membrane called peritoneum in the abdomen. He required frequent dialysis. The fateful day came when his fever became high and his general condition deteriorated. The girth of the abdomen increased progressively and it became very painful to palpation. He started becoming drowsy due to metabolic disturbances. From the needle puncture of the abdomen pus came out. Such infections with staphylococci (a microorganism) spell doom for the patient because infection has full abdominal space to spread due to lowered resistance of the patient. Proverbially. It is said that in such cases even tons of antibiotics are futile.

The agony and pathetic condition of this case has remained etched even today. He ultimately succumbed and in a pensive mood one did not know whether dialysis was good or bad in its implication. My study of yogic sciences has given me much enlightenment in perspectives of many diseases but diseases of the kidney remain baffling. What is underlying the genesis and perpetuation of kidney disease? Some known aetiological factors are long standing diabetes and hypertension, but the gamut holds much more which is unfathomable. Concordant with principles of Ayurvedic medicine one cannot help hypothesizing a relation with '*shukragni*'. Which is the purest form of agni principle from Ayurvedic medicine point of view. Disequilibrium at the level of shukragni may be the forerunner for kidney disease due to genetic and constitutional proximity of the organs of excretion and reproduction. Hypotheses are difficult to substantiate because experimental research methods cannot be applied in these cases and, therefore, all hypotheses will remain only conjectural.

However, it is true this has been one of my academic postulative pursuits to ponder over because the outcome of kidney diseases is so very morbid.

# Case 16

# A Chemotherapy Patient

She was in our side room, admitted for cycles of chemotherapy. She was a case of lymphoma. They need repeated cycles of anticancer drugs. Cyclical therapy decreases toxicity of the individual drug as the dosages are better titrated and the effect of combination of the drug helps in multi-prong attack on the cancer cell to achieve desired levels of cell-kill. Damage to normal tissues is less with combination chemotherapy.

Side-effect of cancer therapy is always there. The brunt of side effects falls on tissues of the body where there is rapid cell turnover, meaning where normal cells are formed and destroyed at a faster rate. One can imagine such areas in the human body like hair and skin on the surface, mucous membrane (the inner covering over pipe structures in the body) and the bone marrow with blood forming cells. Gradually, these patients on chemotherapy start losing hair and become bald. Protection is given to inner tissues with supportive and replacement therapy (like blood and component transfusion etc) but hair-fall cannot usually be halted.

The surprise was the beautiful, thick curly hair on the scalp of this lady on cancer chemotherapy. Her hair was short, but the effect of this silky, luxuriant hair on her head was marvelous. She was petite in her stature, in her late thirties, with some weight loss and beautiful hair, a gown with lace, she looked like a young girl. To add to all these she had an infectious smile. To my imagination, she ceased to be an adult with lymphoma, she was a young girl, like a fairy lying cosily in her bed. There are so many beauty pageants all over the world in modern times with so much hullaboo about them, but the smiling patients are the most beautiful of human beings. They are winners in the battle of life.

# Case 17

# Bhute

Management of coronary artery disease has been revolutionized in recent time. Long has been the journey of medical scientists in this endeavour. Conservative management was the backbone till two decades back. Coronary angiography, interventional cardiology and mutilating, but to a great extent life-giving coronary artery bypass grafting are in vogue today. None-invasive and invasive modalities of investigations have enriched the armamentorium of investigatory medical scientists.

Mr. Bhute's was the first case of coronary artery bypass grafting (CABG) that I saw. He was father of a colleague. Like most cases of coronary artery disease he was a diabetic and a hypertensive. He was advised CABG and was operated upon in a Mumbai hospital. CABG is mutilating in surgical procedure and at one stage the patient lies on the operation table with multiple groups of surgeons working on his body. The grafts are to be obtained from different sites and then these are to be placed in the heart. The sight of the body can be compared to an incomplete building. The finished product is nowhere in view of an observer then. Mr. Bhute underwent the Herculean procedure and returned home. In a month's period he was admitted to our medical college hospital with severe infection of the sternum which is split in CABG to access the heart, underlying it pus was oozing from points where sutures were put. He was febrile with the graph of temperature never touching base line. In a nutshell, he came out of the frying pan and landed in the fire. The sight of Mr. Bhute was pathetic and depressing. Heavy doses of antibiotics were pumped into his corporeal self but the response was very slow. His health deteriorated not long after CABG. The experience could be heart-rending for anyone with emotion and empathy.

Mortality of the body is a certitude but morbidity is frightening. Morbidity may occur due to disease or may be iatrogenic after procedures. In spite of all safety precautions morbidity always lurks as our worst nightmare. Again and again bitter experiences of morbidity of patients have jolted my mind to look upon prevention as the solution. Primary prevention by maintaining healthy lifestyle is invaluable and should be sought after like a cherished goal in life.

# Case 18

# Wing Commander

In the mid 1980s, pharmacologic stress testing and static cardiac imaging for assessment of contractile functions of the heart muscle (myocardium) were not in vogue. With consent of the patient, treadmill exercise testing was done after three months of heart attack (myocardial infarction). This is a way to scientifically document physiological endurance of the heart for advice regarding necessary lifestyle modifications. The wing commander came for treadmill testing after completing a three month period of restricted activity. He was just forty years old. His prior health was good without any risk factors, obesity, diabetes, hypertension, smoking, family history. He was an unusual case. This young pilot was endowed with inherent grace, far off gaze and soft, melodious voice. Over time I have gathered some intangible ways of assessing prognosis of our medical cases. One such way is to observe a patient in sleep. Sleep is relaxation. We never learn to sleep, we just sleep. However, sleep is an enigmatic natural phenomenon of life which rests our minds and bodies and builds potential storehouses of our energy.

An individual of any age, gender with peaceful, calm face, relaxed posture with rhythmic breathing uninterrupted by snoring is a picture perfect, a dynamic sculpture, like in meditation rather than unconsciousness (deep sleep is near to this). Sleep was the wing commander's treasure. During sleep his being was calm in repose and recovery came in with a smile and dreamy footsteps of joy to rejuvenate his sick tissues to health. His intuitive wife, was an inborn nurse who fathomed the invaluable potentials of good sleep. The world has markedly changed since for the worse with most hospitals full of noise of people's chatter, ringing mobile phones, televisions and the hustle-bustle. Those were days of faith in sanctity of sanatorial methods without sound and light pollution. At discharge from hospital after three weeks stay, we had wished him luck. Disciplined in life, he came for follow up regularly. His face always shone with a glow from a healthful state and a calm and clear mind. His facial expression had a wideness like the clear blue sky, a pilot's second habitat!

The wing commander took up the treadmill exercise test with utmost care by an attending team of doctors, with ease and comfort. He was 120% fit. As a student of yoga, this was a real life experience of "All narrowness is disease, all wideness is health." His inner being was clear and wide like the sky of a moonlit autumn night, with a physical being of quiet strength with unusual buoyancy. The wing commander did not have to sacrifice his wings for a heart's little erratic behaviour. Healing is within man, if he discovers his inner power, nurtures and maintains it.

# Case 19

# Kashmira

Kashmira's elder son is getting married. She is a housewife sans all her identity as a promising writer, a journalist. I knew her sister as an excellent gynaecologist. The elder sister was posted in another city. One day as I was examining patients in my outpatient department, Kashmira walked in. She must have been in her mid-twenties then. Her gait alarmed my intuition. As doctors, observation is one of our cultivated and carefully natured attributes. Gait is a very particular storyteller for many diseases. All of us have our peculiar ways of walking and so gait also marks us out as figures in partially illumined background, even when faces cannot be identified. So be it. Kashmira's gait with lordosis (lumber spine protruding forward) and waddle like a duck put me on cautious observation. Such gait occurs with distension of the abdomen due to fluid, fat, foetus, tumour or because of bilateral dislocation of hip joints. She did not look ill so she was unlikely to have any pathological cause for her gait. She was not obese and she had no predisposing factors to cause dislocation of hip joints. Then the only awful diagnosis was pregnancy. My God! Was this unmarried young woman pregnant? How to confront her? How to take the history? Because by the time gait changes pregnancy reaches thesecond trimester.

Taking her to a secluded place in OPD, I carefully and cautiously delved deep into the history and my remotest fear was substantiated. The man responsible for her condition was not ready to marry her. Now was the doctor's dilemma! No time to waste! I must inform her sister and then wait for time to take its toll. Maybe she will not believe my observation as I am a physician and not a gynaecologist. But there was no choice but to act immediately. She arrived soon and the situation was clearer. Some fearless and bold gynaecologist will have to do the procedure. Never have I been able to compromise on this issue, and hence my role I considered over and did not visit them in hospital.

Kashmira got married to another guy soon after, had to leave her job and write an epitaph on her career. At that time she was not aware of the future consequences. She settled in her new home with new relatives and has two sons, who are now grown up, in the oblivion is left the bright young woman with lots of talent and promise in her career. Her elder son was getting married in a few months' time. Kashmira is a transformed woman without much charm, glamour and charisma. She is a woman next door.

Life is an enigma and an examination. We all live life trying to solve its riddle, facing examination after examination.

Our momentary thoughts and actions join like pearls, if it adorns it is a necklace, if it is a noose forms is the question. The riddle of Kashmira's inner self will remain veiled for me.

# Case 20

# Sushila

Our school was celebrating 150 years of existence, one of the oldest schools in the city of Nagpur. From the front rows a stately woman came and bent to touch my feet. This was unexpected. I caught her hands and discovered in that semi-illumined ceremony area, a familiar face seen years ago. She was Sushila. She said she owed her life to me. Well, no one owes life to any human but to the Supreme alone. Sushila and I were students of the same school.

Sushila's medical case was a rare and astonishing one. A stretcher had brought Sushila to our female ward on the third floor on the fateful day in the afternoon. She is a well built person with good physique. It is unusual to receive a patient of this stature in government medical college hospital. The usual gentry is of malnourished and underweight persons. Sushila looked very sick, she was febrile, drowsy, mildly breathless. However, the striking clinical observation was multiple bleeding areas over the skin, the fingertips were covered with fresh scabs after hemorrhage. Some of the tips looked almost gangrenous (a condition when a part shrivels and may get auto amputated due to stoppage of blood supply followed by necrosis).

The clinical picture spelt doom. It was a case of vasculitis, generalised and massive with or without any other cause for so many hemorrhagic spots. The differential diagnosis in such cases is septicemia with vasculitis or some form of blood dyscrasia like leukaemia (blood cancer). Auscultation of the heart revealed a very faint murmur, though the patient and her husband denied knowledge about any heart disease. She had been febrile for more than a week, had taken some treatment. With her condition worsening she was referred to medical college, hospital.

Constructing the hypothesis deduction system for clinical diagnosis the possibility of a heart valve disease and infective endocarditis with vasculitis was our clinical diagnosis. Investigations were ordered and treatment was started. The first week was tumultuous, very stormy. On the second day she had massive bleeding from the rectum. On the third day, she had more ecchymotic patches on her skin and bleeding spots in conjunctivae. Eye examination (fundus) revealed bleeding inside. Administration of blood was to be very cautious as the heart was strained and heart failure increased. Her husband was a very unusual relative. He was present all the time without any complaints or questions ever. A real gentleman! Sometimes her body would react to a very small dose of a new drug. The internal milieu is in chaos in such cases. From the second week Sushila showed improvement and gradually was able to sit with support in the third week. By this time, the thick crests of the fingertips started falling, some taking the nail with them. The raw areas of skin were extremely sensitive like a newborn baby's skin. She was in hospital for eight weeks and then discharged with advice to come for follow up.

Follow up was very sincere, unlike in most patients and finally she was able to resume her duty as a teacher in a few months time. Her case was very unique. She came out of a very critical situation without any mechanical aid whatsoever. Because the body was allowed to regenerate in a physiological way, recovery was complete and also uneventful. Seeing Sushila hale and hearty after two decades that day was like a blessing from the Supreme.

# Case 21

# Kusum

Manav's regards were conveyed to me in all earnestness. He is a young man with a dutiful, vibrant and vivacious wife and a bundle of joy in the form of a daughter. He is blessed with two mothers like Lord Krishna, one who gave him birth, Kusum and the other who nurtured him from the age of four days to four years, Ashita. Kusum's children did not survive. She was advised by some astrologer to give her newborn infant to another woman for bringing up till four years of infancy. Ashita, childless herself, offered herself to be foster mother. Manav has wonderfully watered the sapling of harmony between two couples, Kusum and his father, foster mother Ashita and her husband.

At the age of thirty nine years Kusum was detected to be a case of breast cancer. This was spot diagnosed by me and sent for immediate surgical intervention to an unusually intuitive surgeon. She received treatment, followed by necessary radiotherapy and is joyfully alive at the age of sixty years. Hence the gratitude of Manav for the doctor who he considers as a human landmark in the journey of his mother's life.

The surgeon who operated upon Kusum twenty years back is exceptional. He has surely been blessed with microscopic vision. He needed no technological insight into micro levels of tissue anatomy. His cases usually did not succumb to cancer and metastasis, therefore, because of his intuitive perceptions about minds of tissues. He was an excellent teacher. However, all teaching comes to a nucleus as all learning is seeded. There nothing can really be taught, all has to be learnt. Surgery in classrooms is only the alphabet, grammar and basic numbers. Reality is learnt from life and life alone.

# Case 22

# Mrs. Tiwari

Mrs. Tiwari, an obese woman of about seventy years was referred for opinion. She was a case of breast cancer. I referred her to the intuitive surgeon. Investigations revealed she was hypertensive and an uncontrolled diabetic. Immediate medical therapy was started. She was operated upon at the earliest opportunity. Cancer did not bother her anymore, treatment for hypertension and diabetes continued. A few years later her health started failing. On one such occasion, she was partially bedridden.

The youngest of her sons got a job offer and was to proceed for joining to another town. Mother was not in good health hence the son was in dilemma. On the day her son was to board the train, Mrs Tiwari got up, took a bath and did her worships to deities and asked her son to join. He obeyed taking mother's blessings. He joined his job in time. Meanwhile, Mrs Tiwari passed away. How accurate was the mother's intuition and how formidable her courage to stay death till her son joined. Otherwise, according to Hindu custom the son could not have joined in time. Who can predict, even a death in the family would have meant something inauspicious! Fate and free-will always have duals in our destiny, free will may be just the other side of the coin, opposite fate.

# Case 23

# Kothari Auntie

Kothari auntie is an octogenarian, frail but active. More than twenty years back in my first visit to Kotharis' residence she looked pale, bloated and very sluggish in all her physical activities. Well it was a social visit; I preferred to keep a neutral attitude towards observations from a medical standpoint to avoid even a remote concept of intrusion in lifestyle unnecessarily. However, uncle who was a medical doctor opened the topic for discussion. He had observed his wife's physical symptoms of swelling of face and sometimes feet with slow, sluggish movements. Oedema can be a feature of urinary tract infection and hence uncle followed that diagnosis and wished to have my opinion. I begged to disagree and asked him to include biochemical tests for thyroid function. Many people consider blood examinations somewhat cumbersome as this involves going to an investigation centre a number of times. On the contrary urine examination is easier and hence more feasible.

Somehow, uncle accepted the decision and the investigation was done. Within a few days, he telephoned to congratulate me for my diagnostic acumen. That was very sporting of a senior man like him. Well, the diagnosis confirmed, replacement therapy with thyroid hormone was started and the improvement became more and more apparent. Kothari auntie was transformed from a pale, sluggishly moving individual to a smart agile woman with her new found confidence glowing on her face.

She taught in a school for a few years and with her spiritual mindset attended many spiritual discourses, read many books, and participated actively in several spiritual retreats. An octogenarian she was still upright and independent. Hypofunctioning of thyroid is more common in women and may be familial. With such awareness, her only daughter volunteered for a thyroid function test in her mid-thirties and had the benefit of early diagnosis. Both mother and daughter are living life with full vigor with only some small tablets every day in the morning.

Some diseases occur without lifestyle issues and when tackled at the right time can be tamed and managed, their spiritual mindset has helped them remarkably with medicines.

# Case 24

# Strange But True

Dr. Kothari was a general practitioner with special interest in pathology. He was intelligent as well as analytical and scientific in his approach to medical problems. He had served in the Second World War and was witness to very morbid cases, war casualties. Meticulously, he had preserved manuscripts about unusual cases, therapy given, results as well as his inferences. Like many of his generation, he looked for an intent listener. Not a very social person, he liked us a great deal.

He had a car which was used mostly for social rather than personal needs as their house was in those times far from buzzing city life (1978). Affinity between the doctor who reminded me of Silas Manor and his car was strong. He almost promised to give us his car whenever we wanted. The offer was out of our mind.

In 1991, after our return from abroad, a colleague told Arya about a visit by an elderly man, inquiring about him. The description fitted that of Dr. Kothari. The colleague said the gentleman was asking whether Arya would still like to have his car. Well, as we were not in India, Dr Kothari went away. Later, to our utter surprise, we learnt that in fact Dr. Kothari had left this mortal world a few months before this incident and only after this date was the car disposed of by his daughter.

In retrospect, his daughter recollected that before this date, in spite of efforts the car was in their garage only. A strange event but not fiction! The gentleman whom Dr. Kothari met in Arya's office knew him and when they met he had no doubts about the identity of the visitor. Often people are attached to material objects and that may delay their soul's departure. It is not unknown that snakes often guard vessels with wealth buried in the earth. I never believed these things, but this incident was like an opening in another dimension of the thought process.

# Case 25

# A Centurion

The sound of the stretcher at midnight announces arrival of some critical case. That night the lean elderly patient arrived on a stretcher. He was markedly breathless. There was an electrocardiogram and an X-Ray chest with him. The cardiogram was almost normal and the X- Ray chest showed patches of opacities in both lungs. The patient was taken on a bed, the head end was elevated and immediate management was begun with almost lightning speed for human endeavour. After this we got some time to check his admission papers. His age was put as 101 years. What a surprise. None of us had seen a centurion. When he settled in the morning, with curiosity we asked him his age. He was 101 years young. In life he had never been to a doctor, not even for cataract surgery. His hearing was unimpaired. That afternoon he became breathless while working in his farm. He lived in a village about seventy kilometers from this city. Very reluctant to reach for medical aid, his son brought him to medical college as his condition worsened.

He was a young adult during World War I, a middle aged man during World War II and India's independence. Though financially well off, Gandhian philosophy was his lifestyle, so he worked for his living in his own farm. He said he was a contented man. He expired within forty-eight hours of admission. About a decade later, a junior doctor asked me if I remembered a hundred year old man who was admitted at dead of night on one of my emergency days. Yes, I said for sure: He had exceptional qualities. This young doctor was his grandson.

# Case 26

# Sudden Death

A messenger came panicking in search of a doctor. A middle aged man residing across the main road in front of our colony was in acute distress. The houses had separate boundaries; hence he had to run across the road to reach our place. The messenger's face revealed the situation. There was someone with a massive heart attack in need of help. Immediately, I rushed to the place, after dispatching the messenger to call an ambulance. An emergency ambulance service with preferential right of the road to rush critical cases is totally lacking in our country, with erratic traffic in almost all city roads with all sorts of transports from cycle rickshaws, high speed two wheelers, cars, buses and other vehicles. It would be impossible for even a fire brigade vehicle to rush without dashing against some other. The ambulance service just does not exist for most citizens.

The agony was excruciating and I reached just when he collapsed. Whatever first aid for a cardiac patient was possible was given but with no positive result. The ambulance came after a long time. The fatality had occurred. In medical discussions and academic symposia, we medical scientists present papers about sudden deaths and preventions thereof. Debatable is the issue whether sudden death is good for the individual instead of prolonged suffering. However, preparedness of healthcare providers is essential. Town planning and transport management is the issue of city fathers but with phenomenally growing population and the chaotic traffic sense of our citizens, to provide an efficiently functioning ambulance service is difficult. This is one area where we as a nation are far behind our time. People on roads are always in frenzy, they drive recklessly, zigzagging and rushing to God knows where. Whether an ambulance service to save precious lives will ever be viable is an issue to ponder about.

# Case 27

# An Indelible Impression

Dr. Anil was a postgraduate student in Internal Medicine. These students had rotation postings in various sections of the department. One posting was in the haemodialysis unit. Before the timetable for rotation of students was finalised, they could request minor alterations which would be given due consideration as and when possible. Anil ardently requested for no posting in the haemodialysis unit. As it was possible to accept this, he was put in another section. The incident was regarded as routine. A few months later he was on emergency duty with me and we had some time to have coffee. He volunteered to restart the issue of his avoidance of posting in the haemodialysis unit.

The story was a journey in the past, in the psyche of an adolescent. The incident was an indelible traumatic experience for him. As a student of high school, some years back Anil accompanied a relative of his to a centre for haemodialysis. The patient was dialysed at intervals. During dialysis he was in the unit alone with all relatives outside in the waiting hall. The door of the dialysis room, like any operation theatre, had a view window. During one of the dialysis sessions, Anil was waiting in the hall outside and the patient was on dialysis. Youthful inquisitiveness drove him to the view-window. The sight inside was like a nightmare for him. The room was full of blood and the cleaners were washing the room. His young mind could not grasp the situation. Half an hour later, the patient was announced dead. Anil was an eyewitness to a medical accident. The haemodialysis connection must have got disrupted and the patient bled to his death. At the time of the incident, he could not register the total situation and had no voice to raise alarm against negligence. However, this became an indelible impression on his psyche. He confided that he had mortal fear for haemodialysis and so would wish to keep distance from that unit. He was redeemed of a mental burden that day and he opted to become an internist in his medical career.

## Case 28

# Sudden Death of a Young Man

We lived in a beautiful colony of central government employees of a few scientific organisations. The place was full of greenery; people were lively, sociable with many hues. The Sorte family lived in one of the apartments for scientific staff. Mr. Sorte had a distinctive personality. His face had an arrogant and self-assured expression with beetle leaf colour adorning his mouth most of the time. The family comprised of his wife and two children. One morning, a neighbour rushed to our residence asking me to reach Sorte's place urgently. In all probability Mr. Sorte had passed away.

Entering their house I found stunned neighbours standing in two rows on two sides, awaiting a doctor's verdict on life versus death. Such situations are very trying, the most difficult of a physician's examinations. In fact, Mr. Sorte had passed away more than thirty to forty minutes back. The wife and the children were unable to accept this and that was the cause of those stunned neighbours waiting in silence. Their silence was so eloquent! Acceptance of death of a dear one is very hard, but it is the truth with which man lives life. One is reminded again and again of Dharmaraj Yuddhishthira's reply to the question by the Yaksha who asked what was the most baffling questions. Yudddhishthira's reply was that death is so sure but life goes on without or in spite of the thought. Man can live life simply because he thinks of immortality. Much later, the family history was narrated to me that in the Sorte family men passed away in their early forties. Though a scientist, Mr. Sorte while still alive, did not exercise a scientific temperament to take precaution with strong family history of coronary artery disease. He not only had never consulted a physician in that light, he did not modify his lifestyle of taking tobacco, a definite contender for early atherosclerotic heart disease. Prevention is better than cure, goes the proverb. Maybe this individual could have prevented his early departure from life by timely medical advice.

# Case 29

# A Professor After Head Injury

Prof. Nandlal Vashishtha taught History in a college, some 15 kms from his residence. However, this college was in a suburban town of another name. He had to travel to college on a highway daily on his scooter. He never used a helmet. I knew him for more than two decades. He is thinly built, of average height, vehemently attached to the ethos of India with a fanatic zeal for politics. A teacher by occupation, making livelihood by speech-faculty, he talked incessantly. His being was a vigorous force driven by nature and circumstances. Minor road mishaps had been milestones in his life without much cognisance on his part.

That fateful day, he met with a near fatal accident with head injury leading to coma. Tumultuous clinical events gave way to a prolonged period of rehabilitation at home after discharge from hospital. Their joint family had three generations living in one three storey building in a crowded residential cum busy commercial area of the old city. All family members were anxious to make him well. Everyone played his or her role depending upon available time and means at disposal. The smartest was a younger brother's wife. She was the most educated amongst the daughters in law of her generation. With education came her baggage of information and also self assured manners.

Prof. Vashishtha was in coma, inaccessible by normal stimuli. Most people try to increase the severity and multiplicity of stimuli to bring such comatose patients to respond. In their overzealousness, they do not even think about the consequences of such endeavours. Coma is a form of sleep without awareness. Medical descriptions of coma are in infancy as of today. The laymen are far from concepts about coma. They wish to make their patient talk not realising the cost involved in the effort.

Whenever, we visited them, I told the over-enthusiastic sister-in-law of the professor that television, too much conversation, even too much external noise should not reach the patient. As a matter of experience we all know when we sleep on the floor the sound waves become louder to our ears. In supine position the sound waves are amplified to our hearing. In coma, patients need to be protected from too much, too loud and complicated sound waves. Otherwise the return journey of awareness becomes more and more difficult for the comatose patient. My suggestions were not paid heed to.

Over months the professor regained his physical capacities, but he talked gibberish, continuously. He is now a social outcast and walks about almost like a mad person. Most people will put all the blame on the period of coma, but the more relevant period which should have been managed properly was that of recovery. We can do a lot by having rational patience in lieu of irrational impatience.

# Case 30

## An Accident

In 2004, I was posted in a medical college 150 kms from our place. Every Monday morning I started for my workplace early in the morning in my car with the driver, after a weekend at home. That Monday as a matter of routine I was on my way. As the car neared our destination, a stray dog shot out from the left side bush along the road at lightning speed and hit the vehicle in the front. The hot engine must have caused a grievous burn injury and with a shriek and painful cry the dog went and disappeared in the bush. We stopped our vehicle and found some damage to the external body of the car and the air conditioner was shut off. We reached a nearby showroom where with limited facilities the mechanical damage could not even be assessed. I informed the Dean of my college and reached back home. During unlocking of the door, I heard the telephone ringing, a very unusual event as most of our friends and acquaintances were aware no one would be at home in the morning hours. I picked up the phone, at the other end was my husband from his office telling me of the sad news of the death of a close friend, Dr Shanti. In the early hours of the morning, her husband was driving her to the airport for an early morning flight from their residence, they were about 70 kms from the airport when the fatal accident occurred, killing Shanti on the spot.

What a coincidence that was! Never had my car been hit by a dog or any animal for that matter in so many years. For a few minutes I just sat down stunned to fathom the total situation. Gathering strings of awareness, I called some of our common friends and reached Shanti's residence. The body was yet to arrive from postmortem. In the course of a few hours a bundle rapped in white sheets came which contained the mortal remains of our friend and colleague. Shanti's sojourn of this planetary journey came to an end with a bang. Like her name, she was peaceful on her exterior being. She was always quiet and silent facing the challenges and upheavals of life. Her quietude was often intriguing about ripples of the depth of her being. Was she like a still lake even in her depths, I could never fathom.

One unique feature was her palm. She had marked criss-cross lines on her palm. I have no mastery in the science of Astrology or Palmistry, yet her palm was a matter of curiosity for me. Her life had been very eventful and though on the surface she was peaceful, I had a vague perception, she was not, quite so inside. Most probably she had too much mesh and maze in her subconscious mind. All is conjectural, but a sense of occult haunts to say that most probably energy from Shanti's soul drove the dog to stop my car, so that I could return for the funeral.

# Case 31

## Aroma of Sickness

Meena had a beautiful voice and resonant pronunciation of Sanskrit words. Sanskrit is the most complete language with its elaborate grammar, exceptional resonance in words and its concise and compact diction. Meena, a very simple woman was spiritually oriented. She looked after the library in our local Vivekanand Kendra. Her husband was also polite and pleasant. The couple was issueless.

Meena once called me to her residence to correct some of her yogasanas and pranayama techniques. The place was modest in décor and homely in essence. All looked well, except for an unusual odour. It was non-specific, but not pleasant. I could not pinpoint its source neither deny its persistence. Our meeting ended well. A fortnight or so later, her husband called for permission and time to show some investigation reports of Meena. X-ray of vertebral column, showed an erosive lesion which could be a metastasis from cancer, a bolt from the blue. A line of action was advised and it was followed without delay. She had cancer of a part of her reproductive system with a bone metastasis. She succumbed within a few months of diagnosis.

Analysing the odour, the intangible but elemental principle comes to light. Five elements earth, water, fire, wind and space constitute cosmos and the physical body. The body's energy is concentrated in chakras, the base is the Muladhara Chakara. The earth element gives solidity to the body, it is very dense near the Muladhara Chakra. There are five basic sensory perceptions, smell, touch, taste, sight and hearing. Of these smell is connected with the earth element. Considering all points together, the peculiar unpleasant odour which stirred my sense of smell was an intangible pointer to some putrid disease near the Muladhara Chakra with very dense earth element. Of all energy varieties in the human, sexual energy is the purest without waste according to Ayurveda. In the case of Meena, her being childless could have made her depressed for decades which could have triggered her physical decay. Yogic analysis seems imaginary to many but it is in fact very subtle and deep. Knowledge of yoga gives intuitive vision.

# Case 32

## Abhijit

Mr. Tarun Dasgupta, was an extraordinarily intellectual man. He was a scientist, head of a laboratory in our city. Abhijit was his only son, who was a student of B.Sc. final year. As Mr. Dasgupta had come on transfer in mid-term of the academic year, Abhijit was in Jammu and came after his final examination. Unlike his father, Abhijit was a mediocre in academics. His special interest was adventure in life. He had a very innocent face and a pair of dewy eyes. Both father and son were ectomorphic in build, tall, slim, athletic. Abhijit had no inclination for a scientist's career. He, with his love for adventure, was looking for a similar profession, with options of joining the forces or fire service.

He completed the theory examination of CDS (Combined Defense Services) and was awaiting results when he got the offer to join the fire service. Within a few months, the interview call came for defense services and finally he joined as a lieutenant. Love for adventure prompted him to opt for commando training. During training he had a back injury for which he took treatment and went back again. He also suffered from acute viral hepatitis, but undaunted he pursued his goal. Time rolled, Tarun Dasgupta, retired from his job and went to his native place.

In a few years' time we got very sad news. Abhijit, at the age of twenty eight, was detected to have lung cancer and was on treatment at the Armed Forces Medical College Hospital in Pune. He expired within a few months diagnosis. Man proposes, God disposes is philosophically all right but very difficult to accept in reality. Abhijit, young energetic, full of adventure spirit became victim of Destiny's combat while preparing for combat on the battlefield with mostly unknown destiny.

It reminds me of a beautiful song from a Hindi movie 'safar' (Journey meaning journey of life). 'Zindagi ka safar, hai yeh kaisa safar, koi jana nahi, koi samjha nahi'.

(Journey of life, how is the travel, none knows, none fathoms.)

# Case 33

# Giridharilal

The state of Gujrat was rocked by a severe earthquake in 2001. Giridharilal Dalal, his wife Bhanumati, one son and his wife all perished in the quake, the younger son who was away was the lone survivor. He was a geologist by profession. More than a decade back this family resided in our neighbourhood. Girdharilal was sick with high grade fever and persistent urinary tract infection. They approached me for treatment and after a few weeks he was himself again in health. One evening he came home with a packet of sweets and a saree. I said I could not accept any gift, all was done for a neighbour. Smiling, he said it was not a gift but a token from an elder brother. Amazing is the emotional beauty of Indians, they have myriad shades of relationships, each with its own style and aesthetics.

A near total annihilation of a family so well known to us by a natural disaster is one of its kinds in life so far. May their souls be in peace.

# Case 34

# Megha

One day my son, studying in first year of Architecture, brought tragic news. One of his friends, Megha was hospitalized in the critical care division of a private hospital, battling for life after a bid to commit suicide taking an overdose of some drug. He had lost touch with Megha after joining his professional college. She was probably studying in first year B.Sc. Bits of information joined and led to a clue of some quarrel with her sister, the duo were residing for studies, the parents being in some other city.

To find details, I called a senior doctor to apprise myself about Megha's health condition. He was rather unemotional or may we say strictly professional. Very casually, he briefed me about Megha's critical condition. The situation looked bleak without any visible ray of hope. Physicians and medical doctors are professional with a fundamental difference from other professionals. They have direct interactions with the patients in totality and precisely that is the reason why they are trained to be polite in expression with concern in their voice. This physician was not so on that particular occasion. One wonders, if there is still deep rooted prejudice or bias that women in general and young women in particular are emotionally jittery and feeble minded in their disposition towards life events!

Whatever may be the reality, Megha lay unconscious on a hospital bed with ventilator support and finally life left the body like a phoenix. A young life ended in an uncalled for incident. Joyful, young Megha left this world unrecognized.

# Case 35

# A PostGraduate Student

One late autumn day a phone call from a colleague informed about a doom. Shweta, one of our postgraduate students for M.D Medicine was admitted to a critical care unit with severe burns. As I looked at the morning newspaper, the news was there on the front page of the city line section. Why did Shweta take this extreme step? Why did a doctor take the worst means to commit suicide when better, quicker and surer ways are available? Mystery shrouded the event of Shweta's attempted suicide.

She had been my postgraduate student, only the second lady of a total of thirty students till then who had done their dissertations under my guidance. Medicine is a rather male dominated branch in the medical curriculum. Shweta was keen to do M.D in Obstetrics and Gynaecology but could not get it. Medicine was not her first choice. The reason was she was not intelligent enough to understand the nuances of Medicine, in her own version. With this background we decided on a rather simple and straightforward research question for her dissertation. During a year and a half of her romancing with her dissertation she came across innumerable problems. Finally it was done. The copies were ready. I signed them, the head of the department and the dean signed and they reached their destination, the university.

The hurdle of dissertation over, the postgraduate students immerse themselves in serious studies to face the examination. This was the station where Shweta was when the fateful event occurred. Her physical condition deteriorated by the day with a life and death battle becoming fiercer and fiercer. A friend of hers heard with moist eyes Shweta's wish to live, life's final attempt at survival. But fate decreed otherwise and Shweta died. She was the only postgraduate student who committed suicide. The mystery still haunts me. My good fortune helped me to complete her dissertation much before this fateful event, but the psychological weakness of a doctor has baffled me. What could have been the cause or causes for such an extreme action? She was then 42 years old, married to a doctor with two adolescent children. She was an in-service postgraduate student!

## Case 36

# A Cursed Motherhood Why?

Poornima was in a wheelchair with which she moved around, she had had a stormy childbirth event. She had a bad obstetric history, her babies did not survive. Her mother instinct was thirsty for a baby. During this pregnancy she had many problems, and at last the baby was delivered through a caesarean section. As misfortune would have it, Poornima had received a mismatched blood transfusion, on account of which she developed many complications including kidney failure. Due to many vascular events her leg were partially paralysed and hence she was in a wheelchair. Even with all these problems her only wish was to see her child who was in the premature baby unit.

Poornima, physically devastated with paralysis of legs, kidney failure, and liver problems with jaundice was not at all concerned about these. She was only a mother's psyche incarnate to see her child. The chances of her directly handling the baby were still remote for fear of an infection the premature infant could get. Poornima had to be content with a remote view of the infant.

The physical events of multiple organ failure took full grip of Poornima's body, and on a fateful day she left for another life with the strong desire for motherhood with her. Mysteries of human life and living are deep and unfathomable. However, this case has left my mind questioning dices of destiny with its myriad fortunes and mishaps, prizes and curses, Poornima was destined in this life for a bad obstetric history and unfulfilled desire of motherhood.

# Case 37

## The Labourer

Building constructions go on all over any city. The labourers, the contractors, the noise of many types and scattered building material all over are a usual site. As we passed by such an area the sight of a solitary figure against the blue, vast sky was unique. A young woman laborour was standing on the roof of the third floor of a building pulling a bucketful of water with a strong rope from the well. The roof was without a parapet wall. The carefree woman was almost full-term pregnant.

Such a variation and difference between a flower of the forest and that of a garden. We see so many middle class and upper class women being thoroughly pampered during pregnancy. Many of them become so spoilt as to opt for crazy things during the period of pregnancy, and here was a carefree labourer performing a miraculously courageous feat, unconcerned about consequences whatsoever. She was a wild flower under care of the Almighty. The pleasant and heartwarming sight of labourer-women with infants in their work places is a visual treat. The infants lie cuddled up in their simple cloth swings hung from branches of trees with a day's food stuff packed in cloth bundles nearby when their mothers are out on the fields, children of Mother Nature.

# Case 38

# Leptospirsis

An agitated, angry foursome was awaiting my arrival in the office that morning, one of them was the Dean's P.A. An emotionally disturbed group of relatives of patients are always irrational to a certain extent. Immediately, my reaction was to call for inner peace which is my second nature now. Study and the practice of yoga have taught me the invaluable benefit of inner peace. Events always occur and will go on occurring as long as the wheel of creation moves. Agitation, excitement and anger can never answer or settle any problem. I sat down to give them patient hearing.

A young man of twenty six years of age expired that morning due to severe pulmonary bleeding because of a disease leptospirosis. Leptospirosis is well documented over many years in Mumbai during rainy season, hence the geographical location and the season of the disease had nothing unusual. In the Vidarbha region of Maharashtra State we have not encountered leptospirosis. So, this was a practical learning experience for me.

Leptospirosis usually starts with fever, pulmonary symptoms, sometimes jaundice, nervous system involvement, glandular enlargement and so on. The dreaded complication is hemorrhage and unfortunately if there is sudden, massive hemorrhage in the lungs, the patient drowns in his own lungs and there is possibility of fatal outcome. Prevention pertains to pest control, early diagnosis and treatment. This young man had been febrile for six days before admission. He was admitted the night before and succumbed to massive pulmonary hemorrhage early in the morning. This was the case history. The relatives were agitated as they thought the resident doctor was not intelligent enough to manage the case. He was an in-service candidate doing M.D. Medicine. There are some doctors who are registered for P.G. while on role in Government service. They are older than the normal P.G. students. Most people consider them inferior in clinical acumen, rightly or on assumption. This was the case this time. The doctor on duty was such a P.G.

Thus the second part of the event was clear. I sent for the resident. He duly arrived. With all four relatives sitting in front he narrated the incident. The night duty had been very busy with a continuous flow of emergency cases, mostly of leptospirosis. The critical care units were overflowing with patients. This patient, who was relatively stable, was admitted to the ward and given his treatment. Early morning he had a little blood in the sputum and the doctor informed the critical care unit about the transfer of this patient there. As he was being transferred, he started having massive bleeding from his lungs and afterwards succumbed in a few hours time.

This was the third part of the story. I said to the relatives that the incident was very tragic and irreparable. They could have a grudge against anyone for what happened but what was the cause and what could have been done? The first issue to be considered was the initial delay of six day in reporting to hospital. Leptospirosis is an acute illness and everyone has to act fast. This delay was the first and foremost cause of treatment getting delayed. After coming to hospital when already the disease was in an epidemic proportion, he received immediate treatment. As his conditioned worsened, transfer to the critical care unit was executed but fate had its way. Then what was their grudge? By then they were infused with the peace of the atmosphere and a faint ray of hope was visible. I repeated that what happened was most tragic but could we blame the doctor, could we say whether he was inefficient or negligent? The choice was up to them to take the doctor to task themselves or fight a legal battle. I said, I would accept whatever they decided and once the orders came from the Dean, I would forward it to the resident doctor so that legal procedure was not hampered. They could leave, discuss the issue with other family members and come with a plan of action. The meeting was dismissed with changed scenario. The agitated group left my office quietly.

Days passed and nothing happened. After about two weeks the Dean's P.A. came and was apologetic for their behaviour and mistrust about the resident's clinical acumen.

## Case 39

# Ethos of a Tribal Community

Many tribal communities exist in India in pockets of scattered geographical area. My knowledge about these communities is rudimentary. In a visit to a tribal area spread over parts of the States of Maharashtra and some of its neighbours, our friends (doctors) revealed a truth. This was an established fact from their experience of working in the region for decades. This is Madia Gond community. These tribals were hunters and till late seventies knew little about cultivation. Their social fabric is closely knit, with very basic needs for life and living. The major health problems they face are malnutrition due to lack of cultivation, green vegetables and maternal and infant mortality.

They have time-honoured social practices of their native tribal culture. One feature of such communities in Ghotul culture wherein the youth of both genders have freedom to interact freely and spend nights together, feasting and making merry without any interference of their elders. They find their future spouses after these encounters. There are no untoward incidences if all community members are involved.

They have no HIV-AIDS or sexually transmitted diseases! This was established by our friend's close observation for more than two decades. If any case were ever reported which had been less than a double digit member, the index case was an outsider from the urban civilized world. A beautiful and unique ethos of a tribal community existing far from the madding crowds! Who is more civilized, the technologically aware loud-mouth 'civilized' community visiting malls and eating in glamorous eateries or these simple people living under the blue sky, weather-beaten with scarcity of food, clothing and shelter? They have no hang-ups about free, frank interactions of youth yet they seem to be unpolluted. We do not have answers.

HIV-AIDS arrived in India from the West and is now deep-rooted in metros and urban areas. It is almost becoming epidemic. However, in the remote areas living in forests are tribes untouched by the menace! Their simple lives and instinctive ways are protecting them. Where is medical research needed to find out ways of early diagnosis by more and expensive as well as sophisticated ways, by big pharmaceutical companies manufacturing drugs for HIV-AIDS or by studying behavioural ways of such communities which immunizes them naturally ?

It is an open question for brain exercise if too many pro-active ways are causing more harm than good!

# Case 40

# Dr. Dharmesh

The Indian Coffee House has a unit in our medical college. This cafeteria, if it wrote an autobiography, would tell readers about the whole history of our medical college. There is no place of nostalgia more interesting than a college or university cafeteria. There are big tables with chairs around for one complete unit of a department to sit in the coffee house. The total chairs around such large tables is about one dozen.

A familiar site for a few years was doctors coming for coffee and snacks from the Radiology department. They pushed a wheelchair, carrying a frail fair-skinned man, with a fur cap, his torso tied to the back of the wheelchair with a sheet, his hands and feet shrunken and thin. The wheelchair person was Dr. Dharmesh. He drank coffee from a tumbler with the help of a straw which had to be served to him in the right way. He was a lecturer in Radiology, academically very bright and an excellent diagnostician. Due to four limb paralysis he was physically handicapped but theoretically he was superb.

Dr. Dharmesh was a handsome young man who was a surgeon. A tumour of the spinal cord made him invalid. So he was unable to continue as a surgeon. He studied to get post graduation in Radiology. As he was paralysed, he could not sit or hold a book, so his sister and brother-in-law read the academic books to him. Knowledge gathered thus, he readied himself for the university examination with the help of a writer of course and passed with flying colours.

Thereafter he joined as a lecturer in Radiology and worked for many years before his demise. Physical disability cannot deter the progress of mental growth and development. He was an example of such exceptional caliber persons, like Helen Keller, Stephen Hawking Mary Vergese and the like. Human spirit can reach lofty heights, come what may.

# Case 41

## An Unfortunate Demise

Mr. Banerjee was a thorough gentleman. He was then in his mid-sixties. He lived across the main road from my mother's place. Often he visited her to enquire after her welfare. Mother lived alone after father's death. Mr. Banerjee had a unique way of communication. He spoke with a beautiful voice, in a balanced tone, pitch and with a large vocabulary as well as information. His face had a glow, although he was a cardiac patient who had undergone manipulation of his coronary arteries.

My mother informed me in a very depressed voice one day that he had passed away. The incident was that Mr. Banerjee was having breathing difficultly and little coughs. For these complaints he visited his consultant cardiologist. The doctor's verdict was just minor respiratory infection, bronchitis. He was back home. Within a few hours he left for his heavenly abode. Bronchitis and left ventricular failure have some similarities, but a physician's training is to differentiate the two for treatment. It is usual practice to keep indecisive cases for observation to prevent any untoward happening. In the case of Mr. Banerjee who was a quietly happy person, who was very obedient about medical advice the incident was very unfortunate. For his family this was an untimely loss. The vagaries of human nature are baffling but those of medical professionals can become like capital punishment for patients. Moral ethical values change with time, place and people but a physician's duty should not. It is beyond the legality of consumer courts.

# Part III
## Close Encounters

*To live is the rarest thing in the world most people exist, that is all.*

*—Mark Twain*

# Case 1

# Satyakinkar

We received a letter from home that Shri Satyakinkar Chowdhury had a medical or surgical problem and so he would come under my care to our city. He came, he did not look ill but he was diagnosed by endoscopic procedure to be a case of cancer. Endoscopic resection was done followed by radiotherapy. An incident was very remarkable. A bottle of blood was to be given to him. The blood was donated by a doctor and after laboratory formalities the bottle was connected to the patient. He was in the side room of a ward. I had to leave for postgraduate teaching so I thought of checking if all was well with the transfusion. It was not. The patient was cyanosed with weak pulse. We stopped the transfusion and revived the patient. After this spell of temporary hypoxia to his brain he was a little confused for a few days and then recovered.

He vividly described his experience. That day as he lay on the bed with the blood transfusion going, he saw messengers from Yama. God of Death, dressed in black. They said they had come to take him. Very coolly he asked them whether they had permission to taken him from Sri. Aurobindo (his guru). They did not answer so he said unless they bring the permission, he will not accompany them. He perceived that his guru was on the horizon. Just about that time help arrived as my being and he returned to this world.

# Case 2

# Rishida

Mr. Rishi Chakaraborty was a gentleman to the core. His countenance was full of benevolence and affection. He had been a very bright student and was always the topper in examinations. He was a senior geologist in central government service. He regarded me as his younger sister. Rishida had always nurtured a desire to become a medical doctor. Study of medicine, he could not take up for crunch of finances and opted for Geology as geologists were likely to get good jobs as soon as they were out of university. So it was with him too. He had a dream that his daughter should become a medical doctor.

Dada would come and discuss medical issues, for the sheer pleasure of getting knowledge of medicine. His voice was pleasant, communication skill excellent and intelligence superb. He was a diabetic. For some months Dada did not come. I was puzzled. Then one evening he appeared and looked somewhat fatigued. He confided that by evening he felt severe exhaustion. I asked about his blood sugar reports and medicines. He had continued to take medicines but had not done sugar estimates. I asked him to do that. The report came as low sugar. Rechecking confirmed it. This was a shock, the problem was deeper. I asked him to go for sonography for the pancreas and it was bad news. He had cancer of the pancreas.

His daughter was by then a doctor, married to a surgeon and the couple with their first born resided in the Gulf. The young doctor was still inexperienced and unaware of the world of patients, the diseased and the dying. They came for a family function and were due to return. Rishida had deep jaundice, was unable to retain much due to persistent vomiting. His daughter reported rather carelessly that day that father had retained a little semisolid food. What she could not fathom was why was everyone concerned about a little intake of a man, eating is a usual routine. Such discriminative thought process, she had still not acquired at that time.

Dada gestured me to wait after we were coming out of his room. He asked one question, "How much time do I have?" Both of us knew this question has no answer. He requested me to let them go with their chalked-out plan, but inside I felt the daughter should stay back. She was unaware, almost not caring. Her concern was her family only. Gone were they and within the next fortnight Dada breathed his last. Alas ! The daughter who was his living dream was not by his bedside. The last string of attachment is that of affection. No dying man should be denied this as far as possible. The journey beyond is soul's lone journey, but to see off at the last station is the moral duty of survivors, especially the closest in bond of affection.

# Case 3

## Mrs. Jadhav

Diwali snacks were scattered in large, party size flat dishes all over the kitchen made in beautiful, artistic shapes to be fried. The stuff used to be in huge quantities. Jadhav auntie, fair, short, plump sat near the cooking oven on a small stool with legs spread out. Long back she had a near fatal accident with multiple fractures of pelvic and hip bones, hence this inability to stand for long hours or sit with folded knees. She was a diabetic with severe dietary restrictions. Nevertheless, she rejoiced cooking for her four children and their friends. With so many youngsters to eat the quantity to be made was always very large. None had seen her sans her smile.

As I came out of my ward after morning round that Tuesday I saw Jadhav uncle. This was after a period of vacation. He said auntie was in paying pavilion recovering from surgery for colon cancer. It was a surprise. On my visit to her, she was her usual self, with a big smile. The preceding incident was of a fortnight or so prior. She lost so much blood while having a motion that she fainted. Only then, did she request her husband to take her to hospital. She went through the gruelling investigations and the mutilating surgery with colostomy without losing even an iota of her patience and composure. The surgeons were hesitant about disclosing the facts about colostomy but she accepted her fate with grace and a smile.

She narrated the incident in normal tone and voice. She was an astonishingly brave individual. Corporeal suffering of disease is most often psychologically quite depressing. Some become fearful, some anxious, others very demanding, but auntie was very balanced. In due course she was discharged. Her recovery was much beyond satisfaction, it was phenomenal. The life of her family members was a little disturbed because of this cancer patient who underwent mutilating surgery and lifelong bothersome colostomy. Human courage in insurmountable circumstances has left me awestricken. She lived for many months after this episode and died of a heart attack.

Biographies and autobiographies are in plenty about extraordinary persons. However, human resource in the common and ordinary people is scattered like stars on earth. They leave footprints in the sands of time and mind.

# Case 4

## Mr. Joshi

One night I woke up with a distinct scene that someone was in need of help because he/she was bleeding. The time was 3.30 a.m.. The environment was still and there was no sign of any event anywhere. Then why was the vision so clear and distinct? In five minutes, the door bell rang to my utter surprise. Through the view glass I saw our neighbour Mrs Joshi. I opened the door. She conveyed that her father-in-law dashed against a shelf and hurt his forehead a few minutes back and there was continuous bleeding from the wound.

Application of ice helped the bleeding to stop and all were greatly relieved. The wound was a little deep and needed stitches later. This incident illustrated in a concrete way that the mind's thoughts travel fast and reach the antennae that can capture the waves. Of course, if targeted well the reception is better as in this case. Vijaya Joshi said she remembered me at that time.

## Case 5

# Samrat Sen

Tall, dark, slim would be befitting adjectives for Samrat sen. He must have been handsome in youth. Samrat means king. Samrat fought many a battle in his life of seventy five years. Born on the first of January, he was one of the eldest of the year of his birth. Looking retrospectively at the graph of his health profile it seems amazing that an individual can withstand so much upheaval remaining ambulant, astute and sometimes austere as well. He was now on bi-weekly haemodialysis for his chronic renal failure due to diabetic nephropathy involvement of the kidney due to long standing diabetes. He was an administrative officer in professional life. Social and economic pressures compelled him to live alone in the metro while his family lived in a smaller town. He had an extended family with parents and siblings, wife and his offspring. Needless to say he was a dedicated officer, stress must have been the single most important factor resulting in imbalance of metabolism, diabetes. He conducted his life single-mindedly in spite of the metabolic problem worsening relentlessly. He was a diabetic for more than forty years. Responsibilities gradually over he and his wonderful wife settled for a quiet retired life like soldiers after spending prime years of life at the battlefront.

A great soldier that Samrat had been in the battle of life, rest was not for him. He was diagnosed a case of cancer of the stomach. In spite of treatment his health started failing. At one stage during this battle with cancer, every day was a precious gift for his devoted wife when she discovered Samrat's chest heaving rhythmically with movement of air in his lungs. The six feet, two inches tall frame weighed only forty two kilograms. The abdomen was so scaphoid, it almost appeared pasted to the vertebral column in profile. With prayers and aspirations, destiny changed and he improved towards health. Pranayama and positive attitude were the two major pillars for recovery. After two years, he was declared to be cancer-free.

Samrat's samar (war) with life and fate continued with the onset of chronic renal failure. Kidney failure occurs over years and a stage may come when normal functions are very much jeopardized. This is the stage of ESRD (End Stage Renal Disease). Thereafter, additional medical support is required for maintenance of the body's biochemical equilibrium. This may be haemodialysis, continuous ambulatory peritoneal dialysis & renal transplant (with good condition of patient's health and donar available). Life becomes restricted and to a great extent dependent. Samrat had ESRD on biweekly haemodialysis, invincible in spirit, a real soldier of life's Samar, Samrat fought with mortality and lived on not with a long face, away from friends and relatives but in an almost normal way. They had Durga-Puja in their ancestral home away from the metro where he resided. The husband and wife duo attended two days puja in the intervening period between his two dialysis of that week. Samrat was a living flame, a 'yagya' in life. He burnt like a flame reaching higher and higher, challenging the very concept of mortality! He lived life courageously, completed his wishes and left this world peacefully at the age of 78.

# Case 6

# Mejda

Bengalis have a language with intricacies and lacy pattern beautifully wearing the fabric of language with myriad hues of life, society and culture. Language, I believe, is a flowing river spanning horizontally on the mountains, plains, fields and meadows of social life and also flowing vertically like waterfalls to span time's course. The term Mejda connotes the second elder brother. The eldest is Bad-da then Mejda, Shez-da, Chhod-da etc. Mejda was dark and handsome with a witty tongue. He could create humour from almost any event of life, though his own life was far from being remarkable. He was a government employee, employed in a national research laboratory in Madhya Pradesh. He had one risk factor for coronary artery disease, smoking. He was in his mid forties then, hale and hearty. He was a bachelor and lived alone in his official residence within the campus of the laboratory.

That July we received a telephone call from him that he was slightly unwell and was going to see a doctor. After a few hours another phone call said the situation was stable and then in just about an hour he had been declared dead. We just could not believe it. The cremation was done before any of his brothers could reach him and the cause of death remained an untold story.

The brothers reached there and from the atmosphere a faint odour of suspicion entered their minds. Maybe Mejda's death was completely natural. Maybe there was some possibility of foul play or some mismanagement in treatment. He was an outspoken individual who stood up for a right cause. Then there was always a problem of such astute persons with bosses and shrewd colleagues. Whether he had been a victim of some such situation will never be known to us.

Our ritual cremation with funeral pyre burning the mortal remains is really with cleansing value. Of the five elements that constitute our matter-based body, fire is the all encompassing cleansing force. We had to presume his was a natural death, and I prayed and aspired to the Supreme to take up his soul without any tag of revenge, even if there were a possibility of foul play. Revenge is the worst of the negative attributes of human nature. Certainly our beloved and jolly Mejda must be playing and studying joyfully in his new birth somewhere on this planet.

# Case 7

# LopaMudra

The garage space was occupied by displays of paintings from young artists. Their teacher was a happy grandma, fair, petite with a smiling face. This was a yearly festival when the exhibition of paintings of these mini-artists was open for interested viewers. They also made greeting cards for sale. In 1998, India and Pakistan were warring in Kargil, Drass regions. The psyche of the nation was full of news from the battlefront. Young students were listening to events of bravery, supreme sacrifice by martyrs. One boy composed a beautiful poem addressed to the armed forces jawans and officers, hailing their patriotism. I thought it would be worthwhile to print this poem on greeting cards made by these young artists and send these to the warfront as a mark of our support and solidarity. The endeavour was a grand success and grandma teacher Lopa Mudra was radiance personified that day. In some way that day was very special to her.

Years rolled and so wheeled time and life. Many batches of students went out from Grandma's painting class. In a few years she put a full stop to her painting class on health grounds. Her major feature was feeling light-headedness and fainting after full meals. This made her a social recluse from an actively social individual. Unable to bear it anymore, she came to my clinic for advice and treatment thereof.

The clinical history was like vascular-steal phenomenon, whenever there was vasodilatation in the gastrointestinal tract, her brain vascular supply was not enough to maintain proper function. Rest and supine position helped her to some extent. She also had anaemia, increased lymphocytes in her blood count and markedly raised erythrocyte sedimentation rate, some indirect markers for chronic infection. Correction of anaemia did not last very long, nor did it correct the other parameters. She also lost weight. Two dreaded possibilities were of cancer or TB, the latter being more amenable to treatment.

She was then in her mid-seventies and would not be able to withstand the stress and strain of extensive investigations. So convincing them with pros and cons, anti TB drugs were started. After initial hiccups with some side effects of drugs, she could complete the total course of treatment and is relatively healthy presently, at eighty years of age. Tuberculosis was called 'consumption' because its indolent nature corroded the body slowly in lingering way for months and years. Initially, pulmonary tuberculosis was rampant affecting many elite persons like Kamala Nehru (Jawaharlal Nehru's wife), Subhashchandra Bose. In those days, it was a sanatorial line of management with isolation, good environment, free from pollution, nutritious food and affectionate nursing. The fate of the patients could be dichotomous in option. He or she would either recover fully or die. The society was spared of spread of disease with partially treated cases carrying subclinical infection living in society. Drug treatment has resulted in complete cure of some cases, but not without the toxic effects of drugs. Re-emergence of tuberculosis from dormant to active state decades after can occur. The infection has become more ubiquitous in the body, can mimic infection of any system inside the body. As the medical world finds cures, the bacteria also learn to mutate and survive adverse conditions.

Drug treatment has modified the disease pattern in tuberculosis and the spread of the disease has become more due to non-isolation of cases. Most diseases have some intangible variants as causative factors, for tuberculosis this factor is psychological vacuum and negavitism. Lopa would have been a winner against TB had she continued with her painting classes for youngsters!

# Case 8

## Bibi

Chachi's residence was home to guests of many hues for fun and frolic. The star attraction was their radiogram with stately grandeur and echoing music. Long records of classical music gathered momentum and extra grace when heard on Chachi's radiogram. I met Bibi at Chachi's place. She had an imposing personality. Self confidence effused from her being in a natural flow. She was not beautiful, but her personality had a presence. She was a spinster in her late thirties. Among Chachi's panoramic friends circle there was a gentleman Mr. Akhilkumar. A well bred, well mannered, disciplined man was he and equipoised. He was an eligible bachelor at forty. His bearing was much like an executive, aloof and in his own world that to picture him as a homely man was a remote vision. Chachi was a good planner for social purposes. Her master plan was to marry Bibi to Akhilkumar. Well, where we youngsters could not visualise even a nucleus, Chachi created a full molecule and Akhilkumar and Bibi tied the knot.

A domesticated Akhilkumar and Bibi were my wildest imagination. I thought they must be following full official administrative decorum in their personal life. This I never had the chance or inclination to verify. Time passed. Akhilkumar visited with some medical reports and an X-ray of the chest (Bibi's). He held me in great esteem as a doctor and hence this consultation (I was a professor and not a practicing physician). Doom and only doom spelt the X-ray. She was a case of alveolar cell carcinoma of lung, bilaterally spread. This is an extremely fast growing malignancy.

Intuitive knowledge always lurks as a prompter in our lives and this was clearly visible on Akhilkumar's face. The hope of man so hopelessly wishes someone to do or speak of a miracle. Alas! If only miracles were more generalised. With caution and concern, the truth had to be revealed. The worst issue was the impending suffering in the next few weeks that Bibi would continue to live with. Her days of this life were surely numbered and relentless disease would grasp her in its voracious appetite.

In theory, we know rapidly growing cancers multiply in geometrical progression, but in Bibi's X-ray of two weeks apart this was crystal clear. Her lungs' air space had been violated by tumour growth almost fully. Nature's hidden capacity is unfathomable. With such a terrifying X-ray the person was still breathing and alive. Deep in consciousness every adult knows the instability of life force, but to see Death every minute is the most crucial phenomenon of life. Akhil and Bibi were at doom's door with two daughters. Bibi passed away leaving behind Akhil to fulfil the role of both parents for their daughters. Medical science has progressed in technology, but human suffering is still staring us in the face.

Knowledge about tumour markers genetic information about cancer was exhilarating when I was a young researcher. Now it seems, ignorance is bliss ! Foreknowledge may take away simple joy of living. Who can say that scientific predictions will be right always!

# Case 9

# Akhil

Akhil kumar is a polished, soft spoken man, patient with his daughters, known among friends and acquaintances for his magnificent equipoise. After Bibi's demise challenges of life multiplied and diversified for him. Daughters were growing up. Their education, job placement and subsequent domestic settlement were Akhil's prime concerns in personal life. In his profession he had master's strokes.

He has diabetes and not so usual vascular complications causing morbidity, it is his destiny. Diabetes has two major components; the most talked about is metabolic control. Mostly discussions and worries are about control of blood sugar. The more devastating component is the vascular component which may progress relentlessly in spite of tight control of blood sugar. Akhil has this problem. Small and medium size blood vessels are progressively being affected with the result that his toes are getting auto-amputated. His physical condition is pathetic with gradually progressing locomotor difficulty but pathos is not in his psyche. Excellent upbringing and deep rooted culture has made him a remarkable human being. His being rises above his health and environment. He is not only well-educated but also very-cultured, not only to strangers but in the amphitheatre of life.

# Case 10

# Amar

Mr. Shrivastav was a burly, big man, wearing shorts and a loose vest most of the time. He was a class I officer in the police force. He had four children, two sons and two daughters. His daughter Prakashwati was my classmate. Amar was the eldest. He was a year and a half older than Prakash. He was crippled with spasticity. All four limbs were spastic. He could not stand and dragged himself sitting on a flat wooden stool. Whenever mentally nervous, his drooling increased. They did not send him to any school. Prakash was a dull student. Her father was rough in behaviour, harsh in speech. As he sat relaxing, reading the newspaper, Prakash was advised to read all lessons loudly. She read so loudly, we could hear everything from our residence in front, just across the road.

Amar was a burden to them. The father treated him with abuses and kicks. As I recollect now, he must have been cursing his fate to have a crippled, first born, that too a boy with excessive favouritism towards sons in North Indian society. Amar, with his spasticity could not feed himself properly, but help was scarce. Whenever I went to their house, a deep sense of compassion and empathy engulfed me. I was just about nine years old. Often, I tried to put something in his mouth with a spoon. Aunt Shrivastav was surprised at my actions. Most often I returned from Prakash's house, dejected and worried about the total situation in contrast to the joyful and happy life in our family. Our wants were few, but we got the best of things to eat and later the best of opportunities. We had a garden in the front of our bungalow full of flowers of many hues and fragrance. The backyard had many vegetable crops. We were three siblings and had a wonderful life at home, at schools and at play. Our father, a professor was a strict disciplinarian but full of fun and extracurricular activities for us catering to our chronological stations in life. In contrast this family was very sorrowful and enigmatic to my mind. Amar's father with his gigantic size, rough, abusive language and harsh behaviour appeared to me a demon of some sort, to be scared of. He reminded me of such bad giants troubling children in stories.

Time rolled, Prakash just passed. Her father was always surprised why the girl in the bungalow in front got so many marks, though she did not seem to mug up her books like Prakash. As for me, it was beyond my wildest imagination why Prakash got so few marks. Deep down, there was a nagging feeling that because they did not treat Amar well, they were not happy. As a child I could not analyse more, but the thought persisted with me. Within a few years Amar died. A sense of relief overtook my young mind. In silence, I prayed for his happiness and joy wherever he was. This was my first encounter with a crippled child at home. His name was Amar, immortal. Did the parents know their son would have a short life and that they could wish him not to be immortal?

# Case 11

## Vidita

Our first Nobel laureate Gurudev Rabindranath Tagore inherited the exceptional legacy from his father Maharshi Devendranath Thakur, Shantiniketan. Though, I have never been to Shantiniketan, in my vivid dreams I can visualize every nook and corner of the place. A unique instituation of learning, which resurrected the Vedic gurukul in the British regime. There were no walled classrooms. Students learnt under tree shades, in open air, in tune with nature, birds singing around, butterflies, the conscious flower, flying all over and swinging of leaves with the breeze providing rhythm to life. Shantiniketan is a perfect place of learning in my imagination. Maybe that is why I have not been able to visit it. Imagination has wings, concrete buildings may ruin it totally. It is better for me, that Shantiniketan remains unvisited.

Alaknanda is a Maharashtrian woman, but she is a Bengali deep down in her psyche. She is linguist par excellence and a singer unparalleled. Her father was a professor in Vishwabharti University and the family lived in Shantiniketan. Alknanda and her sister studied there. Exceptionally talented as they were, nurture in Shantiniketan effused their talent. When Alaknanda sings Rabindrasangeet in her ethereal melodious voice there are ripples of joy everywhere, and the spirit of Rabindranath and his time reverberates the atmosphere.

Parodoxes of destiny are scattered in the mart of life. Alaknanda got married to a journalist, a matter-of-fact man without much inclination for music. Rabindra Sangeet was far from him. Tryst with destiny did not stop at that. One daughter was born who had some developmental problems. The child was paralysed below the waist with incontinence of urine and motion. Alaknanda and her husband left no stone unturned for treatment of their child but without much benefit. Alaknanda was all compassion and love for her daughter. She nursed her with utmost care and affection. She discovered that this little girl had an ear for music. This was a big relief to her. She would teach this child to sing so that life would be more tolerable for her. The mother's justified worry was for the physical handicap as the girl could not stand up, leave alone moving. However, she was graceful and regal enough not to stretch the imagination too far in future time, which is not in anyone's control anyway.

Firstly, a husband who was not very oriented towards music, and then Vidita, who was so crippled that Alaknanda's soaring spirit had to accept a limited life of bondage. She was and is a very patient individual, with a musically effusive psychic being. Soaring high, her psychic being was dwarfed by situations in her life. She lived on. For a few years, I lost contact with her due to lack of time for music lessons. I was taking from her. News in a local daily newspaper one morning revealed the passing away of Vidita, at a young age. The humane story was published in a beautiful way. Her husband was transferred. Just about two years back, I came to know of a music programme of Rabindra Sangeet where Alaknanda was going to sing. A friend and I went to the concert and were delighted in almost a divine manner as middle-aged Alkananda rendered her ethereal voice to Randrinath's songs. She lives the spirit of Rabindranath indeed. Alaknanda is not in her prime at present, but the spirit lives on. We often say the soul never dies. I have certitude that music also does not die. Life reverberates with vibrations of celestial music.

Amar was a cripple who was unwanted by his family, Vidita was a cripple who was cared for. Even leaving this world she must have passed her soul's blessings for her mother who still sings wonderfully though more than fifty years old. Life is not a book to be read and finished, it is a brook and stream flowing on and carrying us with it.

# Case 12

# Anjan

Atul and Anjan came to talk about the activities of Vivekananda Kendra. Atul was doing all the talking. Anjan was receptive but less responsive. Rarely, would he endorse his point simply and correctly. His smile was like a child of seven, though he ought to be in his mid-twenties. Noticeable was his intent of listening carefully and speaking occasionally in a measured vocabulary as well as expression. The two young men were far apart. The reason was clear a little later. Anjan confessed plainly that he was on psychiatric treatment and was in a good organization so as to maintain his mental balance. An appalling naïve confession! He was attending some discourses of Chinmayanda in a devotee's residence but had left going there of late. This decision was taken as he failed to fathom too heavy a measure of spirituality. He was comfortable with work and the worship philosophy of Vivekanand Kendra.

Simple that their minds are, they are not often mentally challenged. It is just that they have a different way to approach life events and persons; usually, they are perturbed and confused with fast, clustered and loud speech. Invariably, all these so called mentally challenged individuals perceive the language of love and affection. They do not need sympathy and compassion from the normal gentry but love and affection. In consciousness they are very straight, simple, unpolluted. Their minds seem like transparent glass and not mirrors like most of ours, wherein we only see reflection and less of reality.

# Case 13

# A Case of Cerebral palsy

"Take care, vehicles are coming fast," a sweet voice was heard from behind the compound wall of the building, looking in both directions, memory could knit a story. The caller was Sushmita, whom I had seen more than twenty years back as a young college student. A boy of about nineteen or twenty years was walking on the road with an escort. The boy had cerebral palsy, a congenital neurologic defect wherein one chief feature is spasticity of lower limbs and difficulty in gait. They have scissor gait due to spasticity wherein the legs cross, making the act of walking slow and difficult. Hence the escort. These persons may be mentally challenged with excessive salivation and defective speech.

Sushmita was the same girl of twenty years back with her captivating, infectious smile. She said that was her son. She also had a daughter who was in engineering college. Sushmita was married off by her parents at a young age of just twenty years. Destiny's irony has made her mother of this boy who is physically and mentally incapacitated. Beauty is in her countenance, full of affection, love and empathy. Salute women who have so much tolerance and patience to manage such offsprings. The sky does have invisible pillars supporting it from the earth in the form of such human deities.

# Case 14

# A Unique Case of Giant Teratoma

The human body originates from a single cell with half genetic information from each parent. Nature's wonderful work begins with cell division and then formation of three distinct germ line cells. These then divide and rotate, twist and turn to evolve into the differentiated cells and tissues of the body and become various organs and systems. The play of nature is awe striking although rarely paid attention to by most of us except students and researchers of embryology and genetics. There are three distinct germ line cells labeled as ectoderm, mesoderm and endoderm with specific codes for themselves to evolve into specific groups of somatic (connected with non-reproductive tissue) cells. With creation proceeding incessantly, rarely mistakes occur in the processes.

When germ line cells do not change morphogenetically, they form peculiar tumours, called teratomas. These are benign and contain varied bunches of cells representing three germ line cells. Sometimes these can become carcinogenic forming teratocarcinoma or teratosarcoma. The rate of growth of benign teratomas is variable, may be static after initial growth spurt or very slow in growth. Suffice for the background information.

That patient was admitted as an emergency case with severe breathlessness. Immediate treatment was begun but slow was the response. His physical frame was large and very peculiar. One half of his thoracic cage (chest) was almost double the size of the other, chest movement was unequal and the massive side moved less. On that side the breath sounds were feeble and on the other were present adventitious sounds responsible for his acute breathlessness. This was clinically a case of a mass in a hemithorax. The baffling sign was the size of the mass. It was just huge. Such a huge mass can never be malignancy because cancers multiply by geometrical progression, and a weight of maximum one kilogram of cancer cells can be sustained by the body with the patient alive.

Hence this was to begin with a benign tumour. The patient had grown used to a large hemithorax over years and had never considered the option of medical opinion. This mass was diagnosed as a teratoma. Then the medical question was why this man who had harboured the tumour as a birthmark suddenly deteriorated at the age of 37. Imaging showed that the opposite functioning lung tissue was badly compressed by the mass and thus respiratory difficulty arose with the added problem of bronchospasm (narrowing of respiratory passages). The state of the patient was very pitiable. He was released from his bodily suffering by nature in just two days.

The tumour was found to be a little less than two kilogram. It was a teratoma. There were a few cell nests of carcinomatous change (postmortem findings). Why he did not seek medical advice before is just a conjecture and of no value posthumously. What baffled us was such abnoxious external morphological change of huge dimension was not enough concern for him or members of the family in a world full of people bothering about a small patch of discolouration of skin or of colour of eyes or size of nose! Had he sought medical advice at least a few years back, maybe he would have got the right treatment because dying at 37 becomes a big problem for the survivors of the family. The medical fraternity discusses unusual cases and publishes papers about them but the so labeled 'good cases' are 'worst cases' from the other side, end points to their owners.

# Case 15

# Premonition versus Disease

A grandmother's house is a pleasure-house for children, so it was for us too. We were more than a dozen cousins, with a very wide range of age. The eldest cousin, a Didi was the darling of everybody. She was very talented and liked to do little good things for everybody. She read us stories, stitched our dresses, took us for outings, bought beautiful gifts. Shakti was her husband. He was as generous as his wife. They had academic pursuits, they were teaching Economics in college and then in open university. They were an outstanding couple, loving and caring for each other.

Their neighbour had some health problems and was finally diagnosed as a case of cancer of the urinary bladder. As social as Shakti and his wife were, they were part of every happening in the life of the neighbour with cancer. He succumbed in the event, but the event dug deep into the mind of Shakti. Cancer of the urinary bladder gradually obsessed his psyche. In a few months he developed very minor urinary symptoms but obsession ruled over and as ill-luck would have it, he was diagnosed with cancer of the urinary bladder and died within a year..

Diseases affect a body but are not limited by the body. Spread of infectious diseases is well-known because the cause is tangible. A non-communicable disease can also spread, though in an intangible way due to mental transmission, phobias, rumination about it and too much verbal communication. The intangible energy transmissions are very strong, the wireless system. The phenomena are not yet accepted in science but they are reality in yogic science. Another postulation for thought seems which happened first. Is it premonition which caused disease or because there was nidus of disease, premonition surfaced?

# Case 16

# Sayyad

A short statured dark man, rather thin, face shining with a quizzical, perpetual smile comes to memory as one visualizes Sayyad. His facial muscles appeared fixed in that gesture of a smile, which was a permanent feature of his face. I wondered what happened to the smile in his sleep! It was like a façade of unknown thoughts inside his being. No one must have found Sayyad ever on his wrong foot, angry or defiant. However, there was some mystery in that perpetual smile which was unfathomable. He was a peon and one of his jobs was to fetch official mail from the city's GPO (General Post Office). This duty he did very willingly for one known reason, to remain away from the office work for more than half of his working hours. The second reason was discovered accidentally by the staff after many years. This was the peculiar habit of stealing good magazines, journals and greeting cards. Gradually, this suspicion got confirmed by mails received when Sayyad was on earned leave.

Sayyad had a large joint family. He had created many appendages for his family for reimbursement of medical bills. Almost every month he would submit medical bills and get these, reimbursed. Decades later, it was discovered that he had medicine shop owners who were beneficiaries of these sanctioned bills' money. I came to know him when he was on the last lap of his service in a central government office. He duly retired and very soon was diagnosed as a case of cancer of larynx (the voice box). He expired in a pitiable state, unable to speak, unable to eat, emaciated, weak and dejected. The curtain fell on a chapter of a life.

In Ayurveda, it is an accepted fact that emotions and mentality play very decisive roles in the occurrence of physical corporeal diseases. Greed for material objects is regarded as a cause for cancer. Was it true in Sayyad's case? An unanswered, but ponderable question. Within two years of Sayyad's death, his brother also died of cancer of larynx.

# Case 17

## Rational Uncle

A beautiful house with greenery all around, sprawling lawn in the front yard with badminton court, lotus flowers in an artificial pond in an old washing machine made a picture perfect. The backyard was the orchard of delicious fruits like guava, custard apple, chiku, lemon. The location was in the heart of the city, but impenetrable was it to outside noise due to the landscape around. The spacious residence was pristine in beauty sans modern technicalities. The Gadkaris lived their lives with gay abundance. Uncle must have been in his late seventies when we met him. He was every inch a gentleman with his distinctive style of life. He was well bred, well read, disciplined, erect and dynamic at his age. Often we all enjoyed tea and snacks on the sprawling lawn with children playing all around.

The life and lifestyle was congenial and cordial. One day we heard uncle was not keeping good health. Gradually, he was sinking with not much apparent cause for such outcome. During his bedridden days he would like to talk to me about anything under the sun. The climax of all these discussions was a unique event. He was a rationalist to the core and always proved his arguments by reason. To him, faith was only the other side of fear. Now lying in bed almost throughout the day he must have been ruminating about life, the cosmos and space and time. His aspiration was for faith. The staunch, rationalist wished to have faith and knew not how to get it. 'Life is a paradox with God as key' said Sri Aurobindo. How to find God and how to have faith in our lives is the eternal question and quest for man!

## Case 18

# An Ascetic Wife

Uncle Manekar and aunt had four children, three sons and a daughter. He was my father's colleague hence our acquaintance was very long. Uncle was an extrovert, non-believer in religious rituals. This aversion originated from a childhood incidence of negativity which took away his religious faith for his lifetime. They had great affection for me as for a daughter and overwhelming confidence in my opinion or viewpoint for health issues and issues staring as paradoxes in life. Uncle came that evening to pour his heart out about auntie's attitudes towards domestic matters. A thorough rationalist with scientific, analytical mindset, spirituality to him was jargon not to be touched. Auntie was by then a serious scholar of spiritual philosophy, greatly influenced by Raman Maharshi. One of her brothers, an employee in the merchant navy, a bachelor, was her friend and confidante. Delving deeper and deeper in spirituality was making auntie more and more neutral in day to day matters. She was less and less interested in mundane routine life. She would rather read books on spiritual philosophy or meditate or indulge in some creative work like stitching, knitting etc.

Man's ego is hurt by even a minor decrease in doting by the wife and this happened in Manekar uncle's case too. The dismay was in his coming to me for sharing his pathos about auntie losing interest in family life. The rationalist professor had tears in his eyes that evening. Lachrimal secretions have many connotations. In this case tears appeared from a sense of hurt pride rather than sorrow. We talked at length about life, affection, family, spirituality, interpersonal relationship, disinterestedness and so on. Uncle felt more equilibrium on the emotional front and left for his homeward journey.

As is the usual occurrence, a man feels remorse after expression of emotional disequilibrium resulting from transient loss of emotional balance. With uncle Manekar this was just the result. He avoided any more discussion on these lines. Life went on in the Manekar family as before with two of his sons leaving for Gulf countries and their only daughter, a doctor for the UK. The eldest son an army officer was in the country. As years rolled and the grandchildren's education was to be tackled, elder Manekars became anchor persons for stabilizing the educational front of the daughters of the army officer. The surface life was no more turbulent.

Just a week back auntie passed away peacefully in sleep on uncle's eighty seventh birthday. Uncle had dementia and his emotions and expressions were somewhat bizarre. His memory was knotted and often seemed chaotic and confused. Whether he fathomed the phenomenon of auntie's death was a riddle to the onlookers. He sometimes muttered, they were together. The human mind with a vast, matrix-like subconscious spread is unfathomable unless formed thoughts are channelized from here through proper channels to the conscious mind. Uncle Manekar presented a live portrait of a living form without the proper illumination of the psychic mind.

# Case 19

# She Died Unsung, Unhonoured, Unwept

Father was a professor of English. He was an ever thirsty, intuitive adventurer in the realm of literature which he considered the real mirror of society in time and space frame. Human life is finite compared to literature containing time's wisdom and philosophy as documented evidence. Surely, there are categories and varieties of writers with varied realisations about life and living. And the expression in word form to convey realisations is a Himalayan effort. In this constant flux and movement of the cosmos, the individual is but a floating sand particle. However, this finite small creature of creation is so full with emotion, intelligence, experiences and events. Father was speaking about Shakespearean comedies and tragedies. This was following an inquiry by me as to what constituted a literary tragedy. Of the best known of Shakespeare's tragedies, Othello, Macbeth, Romeo & Juliet, Julius Caesar, Hamlet, it was King Lear which was the deepest tragedy for human life. Father said it was King Lear who died in solitude and Shakespeare wrote poignantly, "… he dies unsung, unhonoured, unwept."

Death has been called the great leveler in whose domains bury most controversies, paradoxes and also dark events. Death with its intriguing matrix of darkness, swallows greedily. Lear was the unfortunate father who worked hard for his children's affection and was finally swallowed by death in utter solitude.

The telephone bell rang early in the morning and the caller was Manekar auntie's eldest son. From the narration, his mother had passed away quietly in her sleep in the wee hours of that morning. When we saw auntie's lifeless body on her bed, wrapped usually, in her austere room with Raman Maharshi's photo at the head end, she reminded me of Shakespeare's words in King Lear ... And she died unsung, unhonoured, unwept ... in her life span of seventy four years, very few people really knew her, leave alone fathomed her. She was very talented, innovative, and creative with a demure front. Most of her own clan took her for granted. She was given a mundane assignment in life like millions of women in India. Women are for service wherever they are placed in the drama of life. They can manifest full potential exceptionally and that too usually with immense effort and sacrifices. She was an epitome of Indian womanhood who departed from this planet to be born again with wish for more value-added life.

May her soul rest in peace, may she get a better life than this one ...

# Case 20

# Of Human Bondage

Children of a wide range of age were playing in full gusto. The weather was beautiful. Their faces were radiant with joy and exercise, and the atmosphere was charged with the delight of life. I spotted a new face. This was an adolescent girl with black curly hair, smart and agile in her bearing. Natural curiosity prompted me to find out some details about this new face.

Rita was our neighbour's relative, the only child of her parents. A few months back she was diagnosed as a case of leukaemia. She went through the rigors of a series of investigations and grueling treatment. Putting two and two together the story was clear. I had heard about this happening but had not seen her till then. She was fourteen years old and full of life. My aspirations were heavenward for her. The school holidays over, children were busy again and they played in the courtyard only occasionally. One day I asked her maternal cousin about her whereabouts. He said she was in her boarding school hostel. This was shocking! The only child of her parents, suffering from a severe disease like leukaemia, requiring much care and caution about diet, medicines, physical activities and studies was sent to a hostel willingly by her own parents.

How sometimes man's mind and emotions get connected to completely remote circumstances. Such was my state. The why of this issue became my search. The answer came to me like the worst shock of my life as a physician. The parents put her in the hostel under care of the school authorities to practise life without her. The prosaic reply of the rational mother was, "We get used to live without her and she gets used to living alone." I have indeed never come across such psychological cruelty. This land where I live always appeared a bit dry to me. I was born here so this is my motherland (Matribhumi). I have been working here, so 'Karmbhumi' but always I found a peculiar dryness and non-cohesiveness in people here. Maybe earth depicts the emotions of the dwellers on the surface. This incident of the cutting of human bondage so ruthlessly by one's own biological parents is to me unfathomable.

Man I thought was Of Human Bondage as Somerset Maugham captioned one of his famous novels, but there may be exceptions.

# Case 21

# Ashok and Anisha

Anisha is my friend from schooldays. We lived in the same colony then. We shared beautiful, togetherness with common interests of academics, reading, music and anything creative that we could lay our hands on. The school years over, we entered college. She did B.Sc and joined a bank. I took up Medicine. Very soon good news came that she was getting married to Ashok. This was a quiz. He looked familiar, stocky build, large eyes, big moustache. His face was a bit scary. I could not place him even after racking my brain. He divulged the secret that his father was admitted in our ward with paralysis. The scenario was crystal clear. He and his friend of similar appearance were at the patient's bedside. I avoided direct confrontation as far as possible. Introduction of this man as my best friend's future husband was definitely puzzling. Years rolled on, friendship continued and acquaintance with Ashok.

Most of apprehensions now gone, he was a friend. A telephone call from Anisha gave me a big jolt. Ashok was having a severe attack of bronchial asthma, with breathlessness which is the hall mark of asthma. His attack was very severe and we hospitalized him. That night was a nightmare. Ashok was upright and his chest was silent, no breath sounds could be heard on auscultation with stethoscope. This means the air movement in the pulmonary circuit is meagre. The patient could be dead any moment due to asphyxia. Astonishingly, he was conscious (the brain function gets altered at such time due to hypoxia). This was his tremendous zeal for life. In such acute respiratory failure, saving life is very challenging. In this case the patient's will and life-force were amazing, and he survived that episode.

Ashok, a lover of farms, fields, forests, flora, fauna, was allergic to many pollens, insects. Now Ashok lives in a farmhouse most of the time because he loves to do that. He led a reckless life with adventures and misadventures but has a heart of gold. Anisha called after a gap of years to ask about some health problems because for Ashok, I am the best physician.

The greatest award for a medical person is trust of the patient, but for the physician, the Supreme is the healer, he being only an instrument in the job.

# Case 22

# Dinkar

A call on my cell phone from a friend gave a jolt. We were travelling. Dinkar, Manasi's husband passed away suddenly. As we would be in the city, we might visit Manasi. It was a bolt from the blue. About a month prior we had gathered as a group of friends and Dinker looked well. A group of us had visited two friends travelling three hundred kilometers by road. Dinkar suddenly died in an international airport in the wee hours of the night before. Down memory lane, travelled memory and the train. Dinkar was a helicopter pilot in the Indian Air Force, full of life with great zeal for parties, friends, lavish food and drinks. They lived in a bungalow with a large open space with shady trees, garden, a badminton court, lawn. One of his hobbies was cooking non-vegetarian food. He cooked on a slow fire of coal. Of course, other delicacies were grilled and baked items. Friends had never seen Dinkar pensive. Manasi, a medical doctor was a right match for him in lifestyle. They have a son and a daughter, both in the USA. Dinkar, after voluntary retirement from the Air Force was leading a life full to the brim with travelling all over the country as well as abroad. He was very organized in all his record keeping.

So Dinker died of a severe heart attack. What was the history, was my search. Sudden death is a fortunate event for the person but the survivors are left with many questions and conjectures of whys, and hows. This history was very revealing. They lived on the eighth floor of a flat-complex. That day the lift was not working. Throughout the day he climbed up and down the staircase several times in his zeal to make everything ready for their daughter who was coming to spend holiday with them. Thereafter, they drove to a relative's place halfway to the airport. They had rich food at about 9.30 p.m. They left for the airport after that. So what is the biological scientific truth behind this episode? With his exercise of the day, his blood vessels were dilated. After eating a full meal (rich Indian food) with beer, vasodilatation occurred to near maximum in the digestive system. There was some anxiety with time-keeping for reaching the airport. His vascular system was stretched to the maximum in some parts of the body. The heart was quenched of blood supply.

Thinking brings only remorse after the point of no return. Dinkar, the man full of life was suddenly no more in the land of the living beings. If only time could be rewound and some events set right, is what Manasi brooded over. "Man proposes, God disposes". Here man proposed and man disposed in too much enthusiasm, reaching a point of no return!

# Case 23

## Madhukar

Our voice is an important instrument for communication. Voice is a peripheral function in the human body, originating in the voice box, larynx. This part of our body is concerned with the final output from mind, thought, to brain, nerves and larynx. The mind thinks, the brain forms speech, connects words with language, situation, person and finally voice gives the output. Madhukar was more than eighty years of age when he felt some choking in his throat and excessive secretions. His age and symptoms warranted a visit and examination by a specialist for proper diagnosis and plan of treatment. He was examined by a senior specialist and diagnosed as a case of cancer of the larynx. Investigations followed and therapy options were discussed with the patient and his relatives. The cancer would need major surgery with complete loss of voice for the patient. Following surgery radiotherapy would be required, which has its own side effects. Recovery would be long-drawn to be undertaken with good pain threshold, patience and perseverance. Of course, there could be financial issues also. The last was the least difficult. About the rest, the patient volunteered to defer decision for a couple of days.

Two days later he declared he would not take any such drastic treatment. He said he had lived his life to fullness and was satisfied and contented with family life. He had enjoyed retired life for more than twenty years. He just withdrew from the hustle bustle of life mentally. His only daughter and son-in-law were worried about his decision, but his better half (seventy-six years of age) accepted his decision with grace and understanding. Madhukar was alive ten months after diagnosis of cancer with routine life going on with the same forever. A Janaka in life!

(He passed away in 2012).

Case 24

# Kamaleshwari

Kamaleshwari is Madhukar's wife . She is seventy six years young. She was a teacher by profession, was a good player in her school life. Creativity is one her assets. All four sisters including Kamaleshwari are very creative in temperament as well as talent. Be it a simple sewing like putting fall to a saree, to embroidery, crochet and shuttle work, craft work or making handicraft items and toys from waste products, these sisters have almost no equal in the vicinity. Madhukar and Kamaleshwari were married fifty-five years back. For fifteen years after marriage, the couple was childless, after which their daughter, Mrinalini was born. Their joy new no bounds, Mrinalini is happily married with two children. Thus the family of Madhukar and Kamaleshwari has contentment and fulfillment. They are a perfect match in classic 1950s style. They are two bodies with one soul. Superficial differences of views and opinions have never caused any perturbation in their lives.

Even in day to day domestic life, they are just perfectly complementary to each other. Madhukar was diagnosed a case of cancer of larynx and naturally the maximum brunt was on Kamaleshwari. As examinations and investigations proceeded about Madhukar's diagnosis Kamaleshwari remained calm and composed. Her being was transformed as though to prayer mode. After the final verdict was pronounced by Madhukar himself, Kamaleshwari was completely in tune with his decision. Once during this period of the storm, Mrinalini told me that her mother had been unwell one night with chest discomfort and difficulty in breathing. She is a case of mild hypertension. When I inquired, she just brushed it aside but agreed to get an electrocardiogram done soon after the stormy period.

We did that and lo! She had had a heart attack more than a week back. That night when Mrinalini found her in discomfort was the fateful one. Kamaleshwari had borne the myocardial infarction (heart attack in layman's terms) without wincing so as not to bother Madhukar in his diseased state and family members. Indian women are really very strong within. They have the capability to take in a lot of strain silently and rise as winners in the game of life. These women, wives, sisters, aunts, mothers form the backbone of our culture and social life.

# Case 25

# Hallucinations

Pharmaceutical agents used as drugs are known to have side effects as well as toxicity. Side effects are temporary and have to be accepted for benefits of the drug on the other side of balance. Toxicity is of many types, some related to dose, others idiosyncratic reaction etc. Mefloquin is an antimalarial drug, considered very powerful as a pharmaceutical tool. It needs judicious use like many other drugs. One side effect of mefloquin is hallucinations. Hallucinations are vivid scenes which are usually unpleasant. During this experience the patient may lose awareness about himself and may find it difficult to dissociate reality from virtual events. Hallucinations may be a part of central nervous system dysfunction with febrile conditions like malaria.

Sumit was diagnosed as a case of malaria. He is highly educated and intelligent. He was given mefloquin. For three consecutive nights he could not sleep. Every time he closed his eyelids he felt his body became light and floated in air. At the same time, he could see his body lying on the bed listlessly, almost like a corpse. His intelligent and rational mind was awake and he reasoned with himself whether he was going through an experience in a virtual world or was he really dead. With this he would often find a few images of beings who were not alive, which caused further confusion. Three sleepless nights with febrile illness made him fatigued. He did not wish to divulge this to his wife, lest she became worried. In due course of time, he recovered and was his normal self again. Then, he asked me to explain the phenomenon. Most probably these were hallucinations and not NDE (near death experience) because no doctor noted any indications of death in the corporeal self. Had such hallucinations occurred with some corporeal indications of death then they would have been regarded as NDE. Many patients become restless at night or during sleep, some may be experiencing hallucinations but unless they have gift of speech and imagination they cannot describe the experiences to their physician. From Sumit's vivid descriptions I came closer to picturising hallucinations due to mefloquin. Without this knowledge remains only bookish.

# Case 26

# Dying Young

The young woman in her mid twenties was in a room in the paying ward of our medical college hospital. Her condition was bad. She was breathless, restless with apprehension in her eyes. Her vision seemed to perceive death approaching her being, was unwilling to surrender. The do or die battle between force of life and that of death was in full swing. It is so difficult to die young and that too as an expectant mother.

The young woman had a very unfortunate and rare malignancy, chorio carcinoma. The pregnant uterus gets this and most probably the outcome is fatal. These cases are fortunately rare in occurrence. The final departure is pathetic. The pathos of suffering, ruins of desires, failed life force were stamped like film on the young woman. All possible modalities of treatment were being tried but death finally won and the lamp of life burnt out, midway in the journey. The impression persists.

# Case 27

## A Case of Post Tubectomy Death

One of the family planning measures practised is tubal ligation. One case came for judgment regarding value of compensation, the woman had died after tubectomy leaving her young husband, one new born infant and another child of three years. Circumstantial medial records prompted that the patient's care was a little messed up. She went to three hospitals in search of relief but finally expired. The hassle the family members must have undergone taking her for treatment to various hospitals with two infants can only be imagined. The jury agreed for full compensation which was really small compared to the loss of the mother for the infants.

Scrutinizing the papers in detail later, a few small aberration in the observation of the supervising doctors was noted. As, a physician, I decided to point out these to the members who are in such case decisions-makers, the gynaecologists and administrators.

After tubectomy the patient was in hospital and a good record of her pulse rate and blood pressure was documented on the case sheets. What they had missed was the fluctuation in these parameters. The pulse rate had risen gradually with minor decrease in systolic blood pressure for a few hours before the patient landed in an emergency situation. The record keeping had been meticulous but mental analysis did not register the implications. Warning signals by the patient's physiology were missed.

Another small but significant point in the investigation was an increase in white blood cell counts with increase in polymorphonuclear white cells (indicator of acute bacterial infection). In Medical college teaching hospitals, simple investigations are given importance for sequential planning of management. This method works very well. Over time, most doctors have mentally deleted this value system from their memory with a perpetual favour for more and more specialized investigation. Thus the warning signals were not paid heed to and the price was too heavy.

In the face of sneers from authoritative administrative staff and the experts in the field of gynaecology, with courage and conviction I gave the viewpoint for their future guidance. What they will register is their problem but such omissions should be lessons for a lifetime for doctors. Modernization of investigations are all right but they are only pointers and not the medical diagnosis. The man (the doctor) has to be efficient, intelligent, coherent in psyche, diligent, observant and intuitive to join the threads to make a complete and correct diagnosis for timely management, or only remorse is the price of all endeavour.

# Case 28

# A Case of Surgical Emphysema

The telephone rang at midnight that day. On the other end was my Associate Professor, conveying the message that Karim, a man of seventy, from a slum area of Mumbai was breathless and had developed surgical emphysema. It was like a bolt from the blue. How on earth did this happen? Surgical emphysema is a condition wherein air leaks from the lung to the subcutaneous tissue. A little imagination will tell the layman that the situation is a difficult one. The air may go on spreading in subcutaneous tissue planes and the patient becomes progressively breathless and in severe cases may even succumb. The treatment is almost futile. In elderly individuals the problem is all the more devastating because subcutaneous tissue is lax.

The backdrop of this midnight's case is also interesting. On a day of state assembly election I got a call from the doctor on emergency duty, followed by a call from the Dean of the college that there were food poisoning cases coming in large numbers from nearly slum areas after consumption of some sweetmeat. By the time I reached hospital, the corridor, staircases were full of the public. We could barely place our feet on the steps of the staircase. With an agitated and chaotic mob all around us and spread all over the hospital, the situation looked vulnerable on that day of voting for assembly elections. With diligent efforts all was managed well, and by the third day most of patients were discharged, in hundreds. Karim had been detained because his chronic respiratory infection had surfaced. That night one junior doctor tried jugular vein (located in neck) canulation for therapy and surgical emphysema was an unfortunate corollary of that.

Giving myself a jolt, I silenced my thoughts and concentrated and gave instructions to the caller. Early next morning Karim was worse. A creepy sense of impending mob reaction could be felt in our inner selves but we kept our cool. With heads, hearts, hands, aspirations and prayers we worked on Karim, with the respiratory problem swinging from one end to the other end to the other for full five days. From day six, Karim showed improvement and in the second week went home. A follow up of three months showed complete and miraculous recovery. The doctor who had tried jugular canulation learnt a basic lesson of clinical practice, the hard way. The dictum is never do an invasive procedure, even a minor one at night unless absolutely necessary and life saving.

Positive thoughts, prayers and aspirations do give miraculously positive outcomes. That happened in this case.

## Case 29

# Fatal Heart Attacks After Full Meal

Human life revolves around a few basic issues and rightfully in vernacular expression this pattern is labeled as living for 'Roti, Kapda, Makan', food to fill the stomach for hunger or satiety, clothes to wear for necessity and more for fashion and a house to dwell in, rarely a home to live in. Civilized man of today is unfortunate to have become a slave of his own needs and greed. His being has shrunken progressively to become a small nucleus inside multilayered shells of technology, information, pollution and commitments. His mind and intellect have become clouded by institutional knowledge, loud advertisements and personnel from management and marketing to overshadow instincts and intuition as completely as possible. Freedom of psychological, philosophical and even metaphysical space is illusive.

The heart, the most discussed human physiological organ is a single muscle mass of the size of one's closed fist. For lovers of romanticism in literature, the heart was the seat of love. For spiritual seekers, the heart region is the location of love, peace and bliss. But for cardiologists, the heart is a complex physical and physiological organ with involuntarily functioning voluntary muscles, the rhythm centres responsible for automatic and incessant rhythmic beats to pump blood to body from birth to death, the coronary arteries supplying blood to the heart muscle and valves of the heart. Phenomenal progress has been made in techniques and technology for looking at and studying the anatomical heart and its physiological functioning. Interventional cardiology has flourished profusely for diagnostic and many times treatment procedures.

However, human life has not progressed to harmony & happiness. It remains parasitic to external support from technology, drugs and doctors. In man, still groping blindly for the ultimate aim of life & existence, then ?

Food and eating for pleasure, more for gluttony than satiety is the way of life for many. Mr. K retired from central government service in due course of time. He settled in his native state with his spouse spending most of his time eating, sleeping and watching television. Both his wife & he were basically rather lazy in their temperament, without any intellectual pursuits whatsoever, though K had been a senior scientist in his profession. When I saw him last, about five years back, he was pot-bellied, with heavy features, vision and hearing impaired. He sat at a distance of about a meter and a half from a large-size television screen, with full volume & visual colouring to gaudy effect. He seemed to have immense patience to watch television without rising from his seat for hours. K got up for food, toilet and sleep only.

About a year back, we got the news of his passing away. They had been to a reception ceremony. He had a hearty meal of Indian oily, spicy, complicated and complex food with pleasure to satisfy his taste buds and shortly afterwards left this planet with a massive heart attack.

Ashita was with us for a music class when we were learning Rabindra sangeet. She is a dark woman with a good singing voice. As we got acquainted with each other, another lady told me that she was childless and her husband was a very difficult person. The information was substantiated when I met Ashita's husband. He was dark with determined jowl and appeared to be stubborn. Fortunately for Ashita, the in-laws lived with them or vice versa they lived with his parents. About two years back I came to know that Ashita's husband had died suddenly after a hearty meal at a reception ceremony of a massive heart attack.

That small, beautiful, romantic, celestial organ called heart gets its blood supply from small arteries, the coronary arteries so that its muscle is nourished to function to pump blood to the human body. The intricate as well as fragile blood supply of the heart can get jeopardised by many ways. One such way is when in a body blood is pooled somewhere else. The total blood volume, its oxygen-carrying capacity and the pipeline network of blood vessels all play their respective roles, working through circumstances, emotions, stress and strain. The gastro-intestinal tract is huge in spread, ramification and function. With massive complex, food, most the physiological functions of the gastrointestinal tract with its companion large organs like the liver and the pancreas the blood supply demand from circulation is also large. Thereby, it may happen as in these two index cases that coronary blood supply becomes jeopardised, with the worst case scenario of massive heart attack and death.

Spiritual seers and teachers always advised people to eat simple digestible food for hunger only and only till one felt seventy five percent filled inside. That was not just spiritual but quite scientific in real application.

# Part IV
## Colours and Shades of Life

*Health is the greatest gift, contentment the greatest wealth, faithfulness the best relationship.*

*—Gautam Buddha*

# Case 1

## A Beautiful Lady

In our medical college hospital, the paying wards are located on one side of the gigantic structure. These are rather quiet rooms and self sufficient as units. A young woman was seen daily walking the corridors of paying wards. She was almost a constant feature for a few months. Her presence was at first rather intriguing. Her expressions were benevolent; she was beautiful of face, figure, graceful and well dressed. Though her appearance was not that of an aristocrat, she seemed well-groomed and mature, though quite young she was in her mid twenties. Her patient was her young husband. He was a paraplegic (paralysis of both lower limbs). So, this was the story. She was the living picture of an Indian womanhood, dutiful, loving and living with beautiful aspirations. She seemed like a character coming out from Munshi Premchand's or Sharatchandra Chatterjee's novel.

The enigma about her graceful attires was demystified somehow. Her husband wanted her to look happy, though he was unable to move himself. He drew inspiration and zest for life from her being thus. He refused to accept the misfortune to be in any way related to their marriage. Most Indian marriages arranged by family elders worked well (astonishing for Non Indians). Three decades back, divorce rates in Indian society were low. Society has transformed since with rise in consumerism and westernization. One cannot but keep wondering if such beautiful women exist as supporting pillars of the roof of social structure! They do.

# Case 2

# Shalini

The medical college hospital had many specialty clinics and one was the Diabetes Clinic. The rush was heavy with patients of poor families. They were issued medicines for a month. Necessity is the mother of invention was very true here. The patients congregated from everywhere and over time they got to know one another, sitting on the benches awaiting their turn to be called by the doctor with acquaintance, new plans also emerged. One of these was innovative. A young man came with two patient cards, one belonged to his mother and another one to a neighbour. He was asked to explain. Back came the reply. It was expensive to come from their village every month because not only did they have to bear the bus fare but also lost one day's wages. So they decided to take turns once in two months to economize. They came with two cards alternately. Though not in rule, we accepted the innovative idea as a practical solution.

In all this hustle bustle, a bright-eyed, slim, smiling young woman was sitting in one corner of a bench. Her turn came. She was Shalini. She looked unusually intelligent in comparison to our average patients. Curiosity persuaded me to ask her about her academic qualification. She was M.A in one subject and was into study of a second Master's. She was in the first division in her Master's examination. This was creditable for a diabetic (insulin dependent), from a low-middle class family and of gender female. Pragmatically said Shalini, "See Doctor, I may not live long but my desire to learn makes me do this. I am taking up courses and would wish to do doctoral research, God willing!" What a spirited woman! Here was someone who was adding life to years unlike most who add years to life!

## Case 3

# Praneeta

Faith plays a pivotal role in health and healing. The science of medicine is like a technician engaged in skills and techniques to carry out procedures, but true healing has a major share for faith. Praneeta was in her mid forties with gynaecological problems like women of that age group. She was simple at heart, obedient and honest in disposition. Her sincere desire was to heal her body without aid of a surgical knife. She sincerely followed her 'pranayama' schedule, supported wonderfully by 'chakra-dhyana' and 'onkar japa.' Incidentally, she is a diabetic and a hypertensive for more than a decade, on regular treatment. With her disciplined following of yogic techniques she improved remarkably in respect of control of blood sugar and blood pressure but waxing, waning continued as far as the gynaecological problem was concerned. Sonography demonstrated a definitive structural defect and surgical removal was deemed essential.

Praneeta was perturbed about her inability to manage without surgery. I convinced her that large anatomical masses may not respond to pranayama and meditation and surgery would not be much of a botheration. Simply, she accepted, went through the procedure of a major surgery and recovered well to the dismay of her operating surgeon. The gynaecologist was convinced about help given by yogic exercises. Till date Praneeta is doing well after, two years of surgery.

The other day she came with a query. She perceived peace as her constant companion. Her face was radiant, diabetes and hypertension are well controlled. Her query was regarding a peculiar state of consciousness she reaches in sleep. Whenever she woke up after sleep she felt uncoordinated with time and space. This made her a little anxious as to whether she would die in sleep. There were no dreams. She felt peaceful relaxation after sleep. A detailed history revealed that as she was a very peaceful individual, she went into deep meditation during her sleep to "Samadhi" stage. Unaware of this she was a little disturbed about in-coordination with time and space on waking. Consciously, sadhaks can go to the Samadhi-stage during meditation and they return to normal awareness. In Praneta's case this happened naturally. The remedy is in training the mind to maintain awareness, to pray to the Supreme or Guru to keep vigilance during sleep and support in the return journey, to normal alert state. This solved her problem.

The phenomenon of sleep is an enigmatic storehouse for various stages of consciousness. When we are awake we are in wakeful, conscious stage, working and performing actions interacting to events and people according to time, place, situation. Only a little of these are stored. The stored information has many layers and units and may be recalled with volition or in dream states. Then there is a large matrix of subconscious state; wherein scattered information lie like stars in space. Retrieval from here is what we do to supplement our information and learned behaviour bank. Retrieval also depends upon necessity, situation, revisit to place of occurrence of an event, meeting connected persons, reading about such events and by hypnotism. The unconscious stage is lower than the subconscious and it is also multi-layered. The unconscious state is deeper and denser than the subconscious. In Samadhi, sadhaks can reach up to the brink of the subconscious and the unconscious. Return to normal awareness is the adventure in consciousness and 'dhyan yoga.' Precisely for this reason, meditation is guided by teachers. Praneeta's simple mind could free itself from tangles of the external world of action and reach Samadhi state with no conscious effort. Such individuals are rare and they need guidance and yogic support when confronted with not so usual questions.

## Case 4

# Euthanasia

There are many amateurs in Homoeopathy practice. Many people have misconception that homeopathic medicines do not produce side effects or toxicity like allopathic medicines. Microscopic amounts are used as homoeopathic medicine. The concept is to minimize side effects. Scientifically speaking, it appears that they work by changing the solvent or at energy transfer levels. So gross actions are taken over by very subtle actions, probably at molecular level. Pawan is an engineer, in a teaching job. He is a versatile individual with varied fields of interest. One of his interests is homoeopathy. He is not academically qualified with a degree but studies the subject with keen interest. He is research oriented and likes to have proof in concrete terms for experiments and phenomena to be convinced.

With his study of homoeopathy he has learnt quite a lot about its pharamacopia. He chanced upon a drug which can cause complete stoppage of life processes without any pain. This caught his imagination. One of his students was once discussing a case of cancer with him. That man had most probably cancer of the larynx and was fed up with his disease, lifestyle changes, in short with life itself. The student discussed the case with his teacher. Pawan discussed about the drug also which can cause euthanasia. The student carried the message to the patient who resided in a village. The patient wanted to die peacefully and became very keen to take the medicine. The student and teacher had a detailed discussion and finally the medicine was handed over to be carried to the patient. The patient took the medicine and within a few days passed away peacefully.

This was revealed by Pawan himself about two months after the event as we chanced to meet him. Truly speaking, I was exceedingly astonished. Never in my life have I heard, leave alone seen such an occurrence. The subject of euthanasia has been discussed and debated from many angles. We have seen and treated many bad cases with bleak chances of survival but never have we thought about euthanasia. Life is precious, has to be lived with or without suffering to the last. Pawan did something beyond his legal and probably ethical and moral jurisdiction. He was convinced of his good intention and his conscience did not trouble him. More than two years after, I have not been able to grasp the full impact of this action of Pawan on three souls, that of the cancer patient, his relative and Pawan himself. Philosophically, I have full conviction about the immortality of spirit, soul. Matter in form of the body is the soul's robe to be discarded as and when worn out. But there is a gammut of time packed events in the form of a lifespan of an individual. There must be some time frame destined for an embodied being. How can anyone judge this time span for x or y? To me it is unacceptable that one can decide to curtail the lifespan of another. This is like a planned homicide performed in a subtle way. Without being judgmental, remaining neutral on this issue has not been possible for me. In the armed forces, killing a deeply wounded companion for fear of the enemy capturing him for information with inhuman torture is known, but in civilian life and that too by an amateur homoeopathic practitioner! Death is an enigmatic phenomenon. Cases of attempted suicide have often disclosed that it was a momentary impulse and they would not want to die now. Of course, the reverse is also documented often, these persons trying to commit suicide several times. But to accept the role of committing euthanasia of an individual level is peculiar. The phenomenon of passing across the boundary between life and death ought to be momentary. It seems that the desire, wish, mindset of that moment is decisive about the beings 'prarabdha' in his future birth. This moment is irrevocable. In cases where two separate individuals are connected, at such a moment there may transpire a volume in silence without a single word spoken. Pawan had not witnessed that moment. What if at the time of final departure, the psychic being of the dying expressed a hint of wish to live!

What Pawan did, he did with his level of certitude but will he be answerable to a Supreme authority somewhere, some time?

# Case 5

# The Child

The doctor aunt and her five year old niece were travelling in a bus in Maharashtra. The weather was lovely and the duo were having a good time, enjoying each other's company. The bus was moving at good speed. Suddenly there was a big jolt. The bus collided with another vehicle and passengers were screaming. Dr. Veena sitting by the window was injured. She had a head injury. All injured passengers including Dr. Veena were taken to hospital.

Little Smita sat by her aunt's bedside. She replied smartly to all questions, was able to tell the whereabouts of her aunt's hospital. Dr. Veena was semiconscious. Smita did not eat, did not sleep and did not cry for hours during her vigil by the patient's bedside.

After a few hours, Smita's parents reached and emergency management was also complete. Seeing her mother, little Smita sobbed freely clinging to her. What reserve capacity is in store even in a small child.

This is an often noticed observation that children can withstand calamities in a benumbed state. However, there remains a lurking apprehension of long lasting effects of the event in the form of dreams and nightmares. Caring for them with understanding and affection helps them in future time. It is wise not to dig the unpleasant event unless called for with the child having bad dreams, nightmares, sleep rhythm disturbances and the like. Smita's inner courage rose to the occasion.

# Case 6

# Mamta

Mamta, an only daughter of her parents, got married at the age of twenty-one. Very soon she was towards motherhood. The clinical signs and symptoms of pregnancy were observed to be somewhat paradoxical. Therefore, investigations were done serially to document at the earliest any deviations. She was diagnosed to have vesicular mole (molar pregnancy), a tricky condition and pregnancy needed to be terminated. With persuasion her parents accepted that there was no other choice. They were unhappy about such a mishap coming to their only child, in her first pregnancy and at such a young age. But destiny has to be given its due. Treatment followed. With a heavy mind Mamta and Samrat settled in their life. Follow-up is essential as it may become cancerous. The usual precaution is to avoid pregnancy for at least two years after such an occurrence. Parental pressure continued for a grandchild. The couple relented under pressure and Mamta conceived against medical advice before completion of two years after the last mishap. Throughout her pregnancy 'Garbha-Sanskar' continued her positive thinking, spiritual mindset, exercises, diet and happy and joyful surroundings. Mamta delivered a female baby in due course of time. More than twenty years after Mamta, Samrat, Shivani and Chandan are living happily. Mamta's recovery without progression to a severe outcome restored faith and confidence which were shaken by the outcome of choriocarcinoma in that young mother to be –

# Case 7

## Shivani and Chandan

Shivani, Mamta's first born is twenty two and Chandan is seventeen. Mamta and Samrat accepted, with full faith "Garbha Sanskara" instructions. Mamta religiously followed all guidelines with discipline and dedication. She read books by saints, Bhagvadgita, Bhagvat, life sketches Gyaneshwar & Vivekananda. She did her pranayama and yogic exercises, ate nutritious food without any cravings for odd foodstuff. Medicines taken were as few as possible. Samrat was very supportive as well as encouraging. Shivani was born, a healthy baby. She grew up to be an exceptional child with an unusually voracious appetite for reading every book that she came across. By the age of nine years she had read Ramayana, Bhagvadgita, famous Marathi novels and was unsatiated for more. She is talented and intelligent performed very well in secondary and higher secondary examination and is a medical graduate preparing for postgraduate entrance.

Chandan is a versatile fellow. Interested in each and every activity of life, be it watching a turtle or tadpole grow in a pond, or frying pakodas in the kitchen to burning a dead body. He is fearless and curious for life. He is like Krishna, wide in consciousness, aware and a keen learner. His fine observations about colour combinations in paintings and embroidery are unparalleled. Shivani is talented single-minded and dedicated, Chandan is versatile, vivacious and vibrant .Both are unique in their types. Chandan is in Engineering college.

Because the mother had a history of vesicular mole we worked with extra caution for her unborn children. My ideas of 'Garbha Sanskar' became more consolidated with an obedient and vigilant pupil like Mamta. In 'Garbha Sanskar' we work at the foundation and genesis level, like Brahma's job. However, Vishnu's job becomes more challenging with a growing child who now has a free will and independent thinking. The work of maintenance of gains at birth is definitely of greater challenge as well as responsibility. 'Sanskaras' from previous births of parents and child come face to face without faintest awareness. This reminds one of Kahlil Gibran's "Your children are not your children ..."

# Case 8

# Suhagan's Visit

Mrs. Mangalmurti woke up that morning following a dream in which she saw her mother, dressed in a bright coloured, jari-bordered nine yards saree, jewellery including a traditional nose ring. She was a picture perfect of happily married Maharashtrian woman in her traditional, aristocratic attire. Her mother walked down the staircase after looking at her daughter with affection. Mrs. Mangalmurti was happy to see her mother though only in a virtual world. This was at dawn.

The reality was clear within a few hours. The elder woman had passed away the night before. As one of her daughters was far away, she visited her though in a virtual world to say a final good bye. Real and virtual sometimes become two sides of the coin, inferences are left to us.

## Case 9

# A Case in the Train

We were sitting on our seats in the super-fast train ready to leave the station in a few minutes time. Suddenly a group of persons came rushing to the compartment and almost made the door of the air conditioned compartment hinge less with the tremendous force of their bodies and huge luggage. They were at the peak of anxiety, like most Indians, fond of making chaos out of any situation. One more remarkably peculiar habit we have is to talk incessantly. The excited group was talking with loud volume, excitement and large content. Finally, they settled the travellers and others got down. A middle-aged woman was in the meanwhile restless with a sinking feeling. One of them had recognized me as a doctor, most probably from the reservation chart. Called to do my duty, response was with calm, care, and caution.

The woman was asked to lie down, breathe normally, with my fingers constantly monitoring her pulse, my eyes watching the heaving of her chest. A few sips of water and the horizontal position seemed to work well. But the male ego of her elderly husband was not very convinced. It was obvious he was doubting my capability as a physician, sans my hospital personality. Gradually, she settled and the further journey till Mumbai was peaceful and eventless.

Almost two years' time had elapsed and the incident had taken a back seat in my memory. One day I saw an elderly, smart lady walking towards me with a friendly smile in the Ramkrishna Mission premises. She greeted me, saying, 'Hello doctor, I know you will not recognize me but I remember you from that day.' She was a co-passenger during that incident. Such incidences are rewards for a doctor.

# Case 10

## Beautiful Bhabhi

She is petite, pretty, smiling and always a busy bee. She was Bhabhi to the dwellers of our residential colony, wife of the chief civil engineer of the institute. In the evenings most of us saw her going for an evening walk with her engineer husband or entertaining guests in their living room. The atmosphere was always charged with gaiety and joy. She was at the centre of the events. Her favourite attire was starched Bengal handloom saree. What was the person like behind this facade? Bhabhi had undergone six major abdominal surgeries facing general anaesthesia at least three times in her life till then. She was then in her fifties. After abdominal operations with large scars, most people avoid wearing stiff clothes. But here was Bhabhi with scars all over her abdomen, wearing starched sarees with pleasure. One cannot help wondering as to the role played by psyche in manifestations of physical discomfort. Bhabhi was so comfortable with all those ugly scars mapping her abdominal wall.

The sixth abdominal surgery was done in front of us. It was a planned surgery for her hernia which resulted from the previous five operations and weakening of the abdominal wall musculature, she was admitted to the hospital a day prior to the operation. In the morning of her sixth surgery, she walked the corridor of the operation theatre with her evergreen smile in utmost ease. Salutation to her spirit which was undaunted by any fear or apprehension, the major reasons for problems after surgery. The event was smooth and on the fifth day she came home. The period of convalescence was uneventful and in six weeks time, the radiant, gallant and beautiful Bhabhi was seen going for evening walks with Dada. What grace in life and what regal personality. Our Bhabhi is a beautiful lady.

# Case 11

## Dr. Vanita

She is a smart doctor, an Ayurvedic Medicine graduate, who works in an Ayurvedic pharmaceutical concern. A doctor's abilities become limited once he or she joins a pharmaceutical unit. He has to learn about the products made by the firm or may work in the R & D division where new molecules are being experimented with. Joining a firm was a definite limiting factor for the medical capabilities of Dr. Vanita. It is difficult to decipher whether she was really talented for the medical profession at the beginning of her career as a doctor. Legally the law of the land gives rights to BAMS (Bachelor of Ayurvedic Medicine and Surgery) to use allopathic drugs, also as in Ayurveda less drugs are at hand for management of acute cases. Their degree has some element of paradox in the form of including surgery in the degree designation, which is also true with BHMS ( Bachelor of Homeopathic Medicine and Surgery). Surgery is a domain of the modern medical science of the west Allopathy. Graduates of Ayurvedic and Homeopathic Medicine have very rudimentary knowledge of surgery.

Dr. Vanita, now in her late forties is ambitious and restless. She has a type A personality, always worried about time and events, fame and power. She came to me for advice regarding her high blood pressure. Her job commitment, domestic set up and personality type concurred together to give her this problem of high blood pressure. Like many such individuals she also had sleep problems. She was willing to spare half an hour for the first sitting of 'Yoga Nidra stage I.' She came prepared for the experience. I measured and recorded her blood pressure when she came. It was high. She was induced to the beautiful and relaxing experience of stage I Yoga Nidra for about thirty five minutes and after that her blood pressure was normal, her being was much calmer. She went away satisfied and promised to practice Yoga Nidra at home. She was given tips of one minute relaxation every time she found a gap in her schedule during working hours.

She came for a follow up after two months and had normal blood pressure. However, such records of high blood pressure occasionally are warning signals to be paid heed to prevent chronic stable hypertension. This is the stage of the body responses which needs to be tended to and practice and perfection of Yogic exercises with discipline and dedication can prevent a chronic disease.

The fundamental question remains how many such individuals will be true to themselves without being observed or guided by any mentor. Self-governance of body and mind is the best governance and the most appropriate. No management is as simple and as difficult as self-management.

# Case 12

# A Case of Shock

Dr. S. was on was on duty at night as resident medical officer in a busy municipal teaching hospital in a metro. A young girl was brought by anxious relatives in a state of shock (low blood pressure, cold extremities, sunken eyeballs and cold, bluish tinge of skin). The girl was in her teens. All emergency diagnostic procedures were done as fast as possible and treatment given with blood replacement. There was no history of any prior illness whatsoever like vomiting, loose motions, fever, cardiac or respiratory problems. She never recovered and expired in a few hours from admission. Dr. S. was extremely puzzled as to the possible diagnosis. Her curiosity overtook her fatigue of night duty and she waited for the postmortem next afternoon.

The team was in for the greatest surprise of their lives till then. The cause of shock was a safety pin. The girl must have held a safety pin between her teeth which was inadvertently swallowed. Surely the pin was closed or else she would have felt the prick of the tip. This safety pin somehow opened in the food pipe and pierced it and impinged on the aorta behind it. From this hole the patient bled directly from the aorta where the pressure of blood flow is highest which progressively increases the size and flow across a puncture. This is what happened in this case.

Wonder and relief both came to Dr. S.'s mental horizon together. The bleeding was internal and could not have been suspected in a healthy young person; hence treatment given was not wanting in efficiency or judgment. Only if the safety pin mouth had not opened, it could have travelled the gastro-intestinal tract to be excreted in the stool. A minor negligence resulted in a major event, a point of no return.

# Case 13

# The Micro-Milieu

A young woman of twenty two came to medical OPD with pain in one side of her abdomen. The resident doctor examined her and because it was on the right side in the lower abdomen put the first diagnosis as an appendicular pain and referred her to surgery OPD. From there she was sent to gynaecology OPD with suspicion of some gynaecological pathology. She was duly sent for ultrasonography and detected to have ovarian mass on the right side. By evening that day her condition worsened and she succumbed. She was unmarried and her parents were not easily convinced that though she spent less than twenty four hours in the hospital, her disease was chronic.

As death occurred within 24 hours, a postmortem was done. The gross examination of organs had the surprise revelation of marked inflammatory oedema on the right ovarian complex and stippled bleeding spots pointing to vasculitis in most organ surfaces of the pelvis. However, the real surprise was after histopathology (microscopic study of tissues), the report takes more than one week. The work done by the pathologist was that of a real master's. The tissue preparations, staining and clarity of the pictures was altogether a masterpiece. All tissues of the pelvis were clustered and the micro passages of blood vessels, lymphatics and tissue spaces were blocked with clumps of myriad organisms. They were bacteria, parasites of many species. The pictures were static but they spoke volumes about the dynamic effect of their presence and ramifying spread in all tissue spaces across natural tissue plane barriers.

Seeing the micro milieu – the tissue suffocation could be fathomed. How with such congested and obliterated micro environment the macro body lived was a marvel. The death of the macro body occurred in hospital within 24 hours but the micro level suffocation of cells and tissues had taken at least some weeks if not months to occur. The resilience of nature is astonishing. Pathology is the science which has made the Western Medical science progress to the extent as of today. The knowledge remains a posthumous one. The final diagnosis is arrived at only when life is no more. As for future guidance the observations are like lighthouses for illumination, which can never be like sunlight on a bright day in a clear sky. The physician's knowledge has to have that edge of intuition to have vision of the micro in a living milieu, only then can lives be saved.

# Case 14

## Problem of Weight

Consumerism is on the rise the globe over. With this has come change in attitude and thereby change in eating habits of the urban rich and percolated to the urban working middle class. One phenomenon that has become almost a hallmark for this is obesity. Obesity has become rampant, spreading tentacles across population groups from middle-aged women to children, especially of the urban, novo rich. The other day two women from lower middle class came to me for advice regarding loss of weight, a paradox in the current scenario when there is no cause for weight loss like tuberculosis HIV-AIDS, diabetes, thyroid hyperfunction. These two women had no cause for weight loss. They were housewives in their late thirties. With weight loss over a few years, their faces looked sad with hollow cheeks, dark circles around eyes. The skeletal frames were diminutive.

On detailed history the cause for emaciation was discovered. They were cases of adult protein calorie deficiency. The food habit in the state of Maharashtra is peculiar in its own way. Most people are very calculating about expenditure on food, curtailing intake of costly vegetables. They also do not relish real salad and fruits. Mostly they are vegetarians consuming just a little pulses everyday with meals. The concept of breakfast and afternoon snacks is extravagance for most of them. Chapatis are made once for the whole day to avoid extra workload. Pickles supplement intake of chapatis or rice and dal. Usually middle-class Maharashtrians have a small size in skeletal built and weigh less. With dietary fads they have the myth about eating sweets which are to be eaten only on festival days or some other special occasions. The total quantity of food consumed is also much less than inhabitants of other states in India. Thus they have chronic protein calorie deficiency resulting in stunting of growth in adolescence and weight loss in adults.

These two women fitted into the typical phenomenon. The housewife's job not legalised or categorised by even the International Labour Organisation is in fact intensely demanding. The pressure on the pivotal women in a household is physical, social, emotional and psychological. Most of them are unpaid labourers in their homes with an emotional cage imprisoning them forever. With all hue and cry over gender equality, women's lib and the like, the bottom line is, the house lady is usually overworked in most middle-class families. The wife who cooks and serves, the mother who begets and nurtures children, the sister who gives affectionate bonding is still a second grade citizen in most households, aside are the grandmothers, whose condition may be pitiable.

These two women justified the situation. They worked from early morning to late night with meagre food and almost no rest throughout the day. They thus spent or lost more energy than they gained and replenished from their diet. Physiologically they were disease free, only suffered from emaciation due to protein deficiency. Myths about food consumption were talked about and they were advised to take a rest in the midday. How much benefit they will get is doubtful because once the muscle mass reduces in an adult it cannot be corrected. Weight may increase but that will be with deposition of fat. If at all such cachexia cases are to be helped, that will be with a diet of gradual increase in protein intake and exercise for developing muscle mass. It is most unlikely that middle-aged, middle-class women (housewives) will agree to do regular exercise. In the state of Maharashtra, observation over decades points towards social restructuring of mental attitudes. Genetically, they may have inherited small skeletal frames but environmental modifications can alter their physique and morphometry.

These index cases stirred my deep concern of decades about the morphometry of the population of the state of Maharashtraa. Like native language and its flourishing in literature and art for cultural growth our morphometry marks our health status. Decadence of any state has many factors, the usual parameters of assessing development will not be able to give the total scenario. When our social awareness and sense of duty supercede our political and industrial priorities is an intellectual and thought-provoking question which needs to be addressed in all earnestness.

# Case 15

# Habib

The servant announced the arrival of a man with a reference letter from the Director of Medical Education and Research to meet the Prof and Head, Department of Medicine. Soon the man was ushered in. He was fair, smiling and of medium height, with a bundle of medical documents with him. The story was of two years during which he had many a diagnosis and as many treatments. At that time all his reports were fairly normal and he appeared normal too. He conversed well and became friendly. Habib said he would like to invite me for lunch, his wife had remarkable culinary skills. Assured that he could consult me as and when necessary he left. He as a surgical case. In the span of the next four to six months he visited me twice with instant declarations that surgeons said he was fine. On one occasion he persisted I go with him to his house for lunch. As I was neck deep in work that day I was excused.

One day as I reached my department at about 9 a., a méssage came that Habib had passed away the previous night in a surgery ward. He was admitted as an emergency case the previous evening with a massive clot in one of his arteries and was probably taken for emergency surgery but succumbed. That evening he specially requested one surgery resident to inform me about his condition. Unfortunately, not his condition, but fate had to be reported next morning. Silently I prayed to the Supreme for comfort of his soul, which was full of joy and hope.

# Case 16

# Sheetal

Sheetal is a practising gynaecologist in her late forties. Her son is an engineer and is abroad doing his master's. She became a widow with her infant. Her husband was also a doctor and they got married because they loved each other very much. Sheetal was a chubby, cherubic youngster full of joy, full of life. They got married and had a son. She joined duty with a baby of just three weeks because more leave could not be granted by the rules. Within a few months of blissful togetherness of a young happy family, there was a big blow from destiny. The young man was diagnosed as a case of cancer oesophagus and died within a short time thereafter. The crestfallen Sheetal looked shattered mentally as well as physically. Gone was the happy, carefree youthfulness and in place was the grave reality of life.

Mustering her hidden courage, which is there in all of us, occasionally called for in its fullness, Sheetal jumped into the battlefield of life with her infant child; metaphorically like Rani Laxmibai of Jhansi who rode to the battlefield in 1857 during the first war of India's Independence. In that war Rani had to sacrifice her life because of overwhelming enemy forces which overpowered her totally. She became a martyr.

Here is Sheetal in modern times, who has lived and worked in the battlefield of life for fulfillment of love, duty, affection. She is now a complete woman as well as a medical professional. With a touch of grey in her temples she appears a picture perfect of serenity.

# Case 17

# Winner in Death!

He had not much of physical ailment. Weight reduction was advised to decrease the load on the heart which he had achieved with walk, mild exercise and dietary restriction, this with basic tendency as well as a liking for good food. On the day of his final innings of this birth he got up at his usual hour, went for his walk to get milk from the milk booth. He returned home, his normal self, took a cup of tea, bath and sat for his worship at the family's shrine. One of his sons offered to get vegetables but he offered to go himself after his pooja and some breakfast. He sat for his cherished time with his deities. The ritual bath of deities was being performed with chanting of mantras. The other son heard a gasping sound and rushed to the shrine room to find his father in his last gasp for life, holding the metal idol of Krishna in his hand, still clasping it. What a grand finale to life's last innings!

To die in the morning is good for the relatives to manage the later part for the final journey. This was achieved. To have cleaned the body is always a thing desired. This was also true. No food in the stomach is helpful to make the body free from excreta. And to pass away without bothering a single soul clasping

Lord Krishna's idol in his right hand is unique. Death is but a passage, and to pass that last gate between life and death peaceful, holding idol in hand is just a state of Bliss in this Kaliyuga, as if Krishna himself took the hand of his devotee!

# Part V

## Technology and Biology

*Fear of death follows from fear of life. A man who lives fully is prepared to die at any time*

*—Mark Twain*

# Case 1

# Doctor's Dilemma

A doctor is permanently committed to saving life. Such has been the age-old training for the psyche of a doctor. The commitment to duty stands on firm ground with little consideration for the human psyche of a doctor. The anaesthetists are particularly trained and equipped with life saving in near terminal cases. Theirs is the emergency squad forever. Dr. Swati, a professor in Anaesthesiology once encountered a very difficult situation. An old man, a neighbour, suddenly had cardiac arrest and she was summoned for resuscitation. Without any hesitation, she rushed to the spot. Looking at the patient, her conscience prompted her to step back. However, the doctor in her compelled her to take the plunge. She performed her task efficiently but felt extreme exhaustion thereafter. The patient succumbed to his massive heart attack and left Dr. Swati listless, weak and drained. All the vital energy of the doctor was utilized in the endeavour. Thereafter Swati was sick for about ten days during which period, she had to draw all her occult energy stores to spring back to her usual self. She recovered from the acute episode of energy loss but ever since she has not been her 100%. Her voice of the subconscious has retained some negativity of the experience.

Such situations are rare but they occur. Most human beings cling on to life-force for various reasons. This clinging attachment becomes an obsession when no more breaths are in reserve for him or her. At such times they may draw vital energy from wherever they can get it. In Swati's case that happened. A remarkable point was her voice of conscience which was unwilling to let her accept the challenge. But the doctor's psyche won over. Such is the dilemma for a doctor!

Practitioners of Tibetan Medicine (The Lama Doctors), are trained to use their sixth sense like a third eye to perceive the subtle body events, thereby judging the outcome of any case beyond obvious and apparent physical signs. In their code of conduct for physicians, when the perceptions about the subtle body spell definitive doom, they can refuse to work on the inert automatum (the gross physical body). Undoubtedly, such sixth sense fine-tuning needs spiritual advancement of the treating physicians. Life is governed by energy of consciousness, the gross physical is only the external façade.

## Case 2

# Voice of Intuition

The surgery of the patient was almost complete. The baby had been taken out, the patient was well as observed by the anaesthetist. Rajashree with her gown and mask was sitting on a stool for the residents to complete the job. Like a lightning flash she gestured them to stop the procedure of wound closing. She ordered them to inspect the operated site again. All were astonished. First inspection drew a blank but Rajashree's intuition was not satisfied. She ordered a pair of surgical gloves, went to the patient on the table and searched again. The voice of intuition was right. A small blood soaked mop was discovered and thereafter the wound was sutured. The flash of intuition vanished just as quickly as it had arrived. Intuition is the superior intelligence from which information can be drawn if one has deep inner silence and is able to listen to the momentary flash.

She looked with gratitude at Rajashree. Her eyelids were drooping as though withdrawing from this world. She was a case of HIV AIDS who was pregnant but labour did not proceed and she was exhausted. Silently she was pleading for help in the process of childbirth. Duty doctors rotated and they left her to her fate. Rajashree reported for her emergency duty and this critical patient was waiting for her. Intuitive as she is, realisation came to her that the baby has to be removed or else the woman will not be able to die in peace. She helped the dying HIV AIDS patient and delivered the stilborn. The patient left this world with gratitude and peace.

# Case 3

# Khushboo

Rewati is the eldest of five daughters of Nandlal Awasthi, whose wife had to undergo six pregnancies for begetting a son. Fortune favoured Mrs. Awasthi for all their daughters were fair in complexion and beautiful in face as well as form. They were very well brought up. Hence there was no problem in matrimonial matters for the elder four daughters. The issue of the fifth daughter Uma is unique. Rewati was married to a handsome young man settled in a big city in the state of Rajasthan. All four daughters of Nandlal Awasthi were married without any dowry. Rewati soon became an Indian docile housewife with numerous relatives all around her. I met Rewati almost ten years after her marriage. She was at her parents' place for her third childbirth. The mood in the household was of tension, an underlying deep rooted sorrow looming large.

Initiating some social conversation, I learnt Rewati had lost her two children in their infancy. Both had suffered from jaundice. Frustration with destiny often leads people to find unjustified reasons for mishaps in their lives. Rewati and her parents believed that some witchcraft was responsible for the death of her infants. The person under suspicious scrutiny was a co-sister of Rewati who had probably no son. The coincidence of two toddlers dying of jaundice was a pointer to some genetic cause for the occurrence which was as yet difficult for them to grasp.

However, what was agreed upon was to have the next baby thoroughly investigated as early as possible and feasible after birth for any genetic problem to be corrected by proper treatment. In due course of time, Rewati gave birth to a beautiful girl who was christened Khushboo. The baby was referred to a paediatrician and investigated. Diagnosis was achieved. She was a case of Wilson's disease, a genetic disease of copper metabolism which results in liver disease, nervous system involvement and if not treated can be fatal. The mystery and myth of Rewati's two infants dying with jaundice was thus scientifically solved. However complex and caged as the human mind is, I am not sure her parents were convinced. Khushboo was left with her grandparents as an infant to be away from her own home. But the desire for a male child persisted as submerged fire. Rewati was pregnant again when Khushboo was four, five years old. Science has advanced, but where is the scientific man, one wonders. Rewati delivered twins. They also have Wilson's disease. One of the twins, a boy, has already received live transplant for advancing liver damage due to the genetic disease.

On May 25, 2010, Khushboo died of cirrhosis of the liver (from Wilson's disease) and complications thereof, she was in her teens. Appalling is the mindset! So many lives wasted, still the family is unable to accept and follow a different route in life (adoption rather than begetting children who are to suffer and die young).

## Case 4

# Of Human Aspiration, Belief, Fate and Effort

One major problem which does not evoke much concern from polity in India is population. The issue has taken a back seat and is not addressed anymore. It is a boon to have a populous nation for the vote bank. Female foeticide erupts as news occasionally but in the subterranean region of the social milieu it must be still functional. The majority of Indians still have intense and passionate desire for sons. Nandlal and his wife were like average Indian couples in their psyche. Every time the wife conceived they left no stone unturned for a son, following any rituals or offering to deities anyone suggested. They had four daughters by then. Mrs Nandlal conceived for the fifth time. Throughout the period of pregnancy her aspiration was for a son, her belief was for a son but fate's decree was otherwise. A pretty daughter was born. Incidentally, all their daughters are good looking. The girl grew up, was bright in academics and tomboyish in attitude. She graduated to become an engineer.

The mother's psyche during pregnancy, however, left a permanent mark on the girl. Phenotypically, she is female but masculine in attitude, pretty and bright in appearance sans the physiological indicators of female gender. She lacks developmental growth of the reproductive system and never attained menarche. Aspiration not fulfilled, Mr. and Mrs. Awasthi took a sixth chance for a son. A son was born in due course of time calling for grand celebrations and fanfare. But the son has neither the good looks of his sisters, nor is he as bright academically like his engineer sister.

Man proposes, God disposes, but many times man cannot accept destiny beyond effort and human shortsightedness. At such times he may pick up a wrong option, of the available many. Maybe here we find reason for not getting spiritual giants like Shankaracharya whose parents, when given the choice of having a child with average intelligence and longevity versus an extraordinary genius with short lifespan, chose the latter option. Spiritual pathfinders have come through usual birth cycles but with different aspirations, beliefs and efforts of parents to be. One cannot help linking philosophically to Bhagvadgita, aspiration, belief, effort and choice of destiny are in our hands, the fruit is to be left to the Supreme's will.

# Case 5

# A Case of Valve Replacement

Nandu was diagnosed as a case of rheumatic vabular heart disease. This affects children and adolescents and is the leading cause of cardiovascular disease in childhood and adolescence. Nandu was from a rural background. His mother lived in the city for education of the children. The father was in the village. The parents were not on amiable terms. For Nandu's treatment, the father agreed to spend on medical expenses.

His aortic valve needed a replacement. This valve is located between a muscular left ventricle of the heart and the aorta, the major blood vessel carrying blood to the body with high pressure from its walls to propel blood to the remotest parts of the body. Nandu was sent to Mumbai and valve replacement surgery was performed successfully. He was on follow up and did well in the post-operative period and also subsequently. He joined a job and when I saw him almost eight years after valve surgery, he looked rather sturdy, for his heart disease. My physician's advice to him was to mind his weight to save his heart from more burden. He expressed a wish to get married. This proposal I could not accept whole-heartedly as the aortic valve was already eight years old. The best function of a replaced valve is on an average for ten years. There was no problem then but should one willingly take a step towards going ahead with family life could be a debatable issue.

Marriage for the sake of love, with complete clean breast about the depth of the problem, with mature and pragmatic decision regarding procreation could be the choicest alternative. However, in India, common people marry at a particular age, to live a family life for settlement and procreation, consider love as almost a utopian issue. Then what about the practical viewpoint? Without being harsh, the matter was discussed with Nandu and his mother, but the social ideas overruled rational and scientific opinions. He got married. Within six months, Nandu was again having problems of heart failure and the young pregnant wife was following him to doctors and hospitals. Vanished was their happiness of family life with a child yet to be born. This continued for a period of a few months. Re-replacement of the valve was considered with a lot of skepticism. And the final blow came like a big storm. Nandu expired.

His wife lives, working as a teacher in a school, a single parent to their son who is about thirteen years of age. What an enigma in life! Miscalculation? Hoping against hope? Or adamancy and foolishness to accept reality? A question to ponder is why is marriage a necessity for everyone irrespective of health issues? This is India, where people live in the twentieth century and have a mindset of at least two centuries back in the past. Individual lives become victim of social taboos without rhyme or reason.

# Case 6

# The Jargon of Transplantation

Administrative duties for heads of departments in medical colleges, encompass many committee meetings like those for academics, patient care, medicolegal cases and so on. As head of the Department of Internal Medicine, one such committee was for kidney transplant. The other members of the committee were the heads of the departments of Surgery, Pharmacology, Nephrology, the Medical Superintendant of the hospital. The scrutiny is for proper identification of the patient in need of kidney transplant, the medical details, demographic and social data and the prospective donor. In government set up only relatives can act as donor. The patients are from poor socio-economic background, coming from geographically far off places, rural interiors of the state and neighbouring states.

The pathetic state of the patients, the pathos of the relatives form a web of poverty-stricken congregations of rural India. With most facilities made available at subsidized rates, they are required to pool resources for a financial burden of almost one lac rupees which is an astronomical sum for that class of people. They often sell off their land, house (or mortgaged this). But what we questioned ourselves was for what goal? Even if the patient did receive a good transplanted organ and fared reasonably well in immediate post transplant phase, he would be a liability and a financial burden for the rest of his lifc.

As committee members our duty is to look at the academic and scientific merits of the cases and certify for further proceedings. In our hearts we are not able to accept this morally. We try to put plain facts in as clear terms as we can within our administrative jurisdiction to the aspirant relatives about the flip side of the issue. Their emotional tidings are so strong that they do not relent. The most crucial was the case of a non-blood-relative donor, the young wife of the patient with two small children to be looked after. She was very insistent to be a donor. In spite of our whole-hearted effort to make her see the problem in light of the patients future liability and the bringing up of the children she did not relent. We had to give a grudging nod. However, to our relief, maybe to the prospective donor's despair, HLA matching failed and she was not accepted as a donor.

The thought chain goes far into the poverty ridden millions for whom technological boon is just a utopian idea, but the gluing force is their emotional bonding to life and living. Technology may have added a few quantitative years to the lives of a few people but the qualitative life-years are added only by that bonding. Jai Ho!

# Case 7

# Effects of Heroic Lung Resection

Within the jurisdiction of administrative duties of heads of clinical departments, one of the painstaking issues is to be on the seats of judges for analysis of some treatments instituted by other medical colleagues with unwanted outcomes. A case came to one such committee of which I was a jury member. This was a very unusual case. A doctor patient, probably an NRI in some Gulf country was diagnosed as a case of lung cancer. He was treated a year and a half back before the event and went back. This time he came for follow up, was ambulant without much complaint as per records. Only one relative, a sister who was also a doctor accompanied him. He was operated upon in some private centre and died in 72 hours of the surgery. The sister complained that surgery was the cause of death and it was not necessary.

The surgical procedure had been of multiple wedge-resections from lung tissue which had metastases from cancer. Many wedges were resected. The patient died within three day of surgery. The surgical procedure to our minds was too drastic and extensive for the physiological systems of the patient to cope up. The chief thoracic surgeon was summoned for direct questioning. He came well prepared with CDs of surgical procedure of the case in question and of other cases he had successfully operated upon and also print-outs of references of such surgical procedures from other cardiothoracic centres of the world.

Scientifically and technically evidence was there to justify the heroic surgical resections so the surgical team could not be blamed either for lack of experience or negligence but for the patient's family the loss was irrevocable. Jury decision of such cases is very paradoxical in the sense that scientific data has not resulted in cure or survival but in fatality. What remains unsaid or submerged is the real motive of the health care providers. The voice of their conscience must be their real judge.

# Case 8

# Death of the Terrorist

The court verdicts about many terrorists on trial for the Mumbai bomb blasts were constantly in the news. There were many names with their photographs with details about their crimes and the punishments awarded to them. Missing was the name of one of their leaders, a huge man who often got admitted to the Prisoners' ward in our medical college hospital. His frame was so large, the wheelchairs and stretchers were small for him. What happened to his fate remained unknown to me and so I called one of my juniors still in the college to find out. She said he had died in the hospital of heart attack.

Down memory lane came the first picture of this giant of a human being. He was in a wheelchair which was being pushed by two attendants as one alone could not do so. My associate professor told me he was a master criminal of the bomb blast and was a fearsome individual. He had diabetes mellitus, cataracts and vision problems due to retinal damage. This was my first direct encounter with a real terrorist. From a distance I picturised his physical frame and sent my aspirations upward for the Supreme to give me compassion to deal with him. All prisoners were under care of the heads of respective departments. The prisoners' ward is in an isolated building on the third floor with more policemen on duty than the number of prisoner patients. The entrance gatc had a double locking system with registers in front to be signed before entering even for doctors.

Searching deep inside my own psyche I could detect no trace of fear. More than a decade back, I was pensive about terrorism and terrorists and over a few days of churning within I felt terrorists should not be hated, terrorism should be, reminding me of a beautiful excerpt from the Bible often narrated in school prayers, "Hate the sin, not the sinner." For me journey into my own psyche was a practical aspect of the theory therein. I was convinced that I had no fear. One evening we got an urgent call, from the prisoners' ward that they had declared hunger strike to protest against some of their grievances being not solved by authorities. My associated professor, a lady of 158 cms and 60 kg and myself 150 cms and 50 kg reached the Prisoners' ward. Straight we went to Izaz, the big man, their leader to find out from the patient what the matter was. He was very polite and good mannered in his speech betraying any seal of cruelty or terrorism on his psyche.

With calm, composure on my countenance, I addressed him as a brother and asked him what the issue was. He complained that for three days sweepers had not come to clean the toilets and the dresser had not come for dressing of surgical patients. They had registered their grievances in the morning but as nothing happened in a positive direction, they had declared hunger strike. With real sympathy in my voice and composure an my countenance I requested them to partake food. We promised that personally we would see to the cleanliness next morning. Late that night they accepted to withdraw their hunger strike and ate. After more than two years the picture of the giant frame of the branded terrorist speaking with manners and etiquette still stands in my visual imagery, and what a surprise that Destiny decided to give him a natural death than the gallows of human police and law. The greatest and the most impartial judge sits there above directing life and existence.

Case 9

# Return of the Native

The world has become a global village, courtesy of technological advance in communication and travel. Life has become fast, more pervasive across distances by land, water or air. This phenomenon is awesome for man's mind, intellect and psyche. Many youngsters nurture a secret desire to go abroad for education, employment or both. Soon our country may become an old-age home and maybe we will see more foreigners from poorer nations roaming our streets and studying in our educational institutions. But who will even venture to even ponder over such a scenario. Time is a scarce commodity, always in limited supply. To be busy is fashionable even in a make believe way. The elite parents send their wards to study abroad on the slightest of pretexts.

Anubhav, son of a professor in a prestigious Management institute was studying in the USA for about one year. He came to his home town for a brief vacation, which usually becomes a period of intense activity, travels and feasting and pleasure seeking. Anubhav's vacation time also flew fast and he returned to the States. Within a few day he was gripped by liver infection (viral hepatitis). This is of uncommon occurrence in developed countries. In an overzealous treatment and investigation schedule, the young man went through innumerable investigations and heroic treatment measures. His liver functions deteriorated progressively and with nervous system failure, the patient landed in hepatic coma. A partial live transplantation was also done but the life-force got released from his corporeal tenament. The parents had to rush to bring back the mortal remains of the young student who had barely entered adulthood. The native of the country returned! But in what state!

Agrarian life changed to industrial and mechanical life for mankind with gradual but almost persistent loss of sense of belonging to our family, our parents, our motherland. Most of the elite sit idly in comfortable and cosy living rooms of plush bungalows and casually discuss the follies of fellow-countrymen, turn a cynical glance at the poor, dirty, filthy dwellers of nearby slums, criticize the caste-reservation system, then drink their glasses of high-quality liquor and disperse to lie on soft beds with or without natural sleep. Who is really willing to do something, to even consider other options? Man is losing native belonging. Heaven is too far high above, almost a phoenix, inaccessible, hell is too fearsome and native, mother-earth we have exploited ruthlessly so it may turn like an imaginary hell. Where are we natives of? Where do we belong? Modern man, a slave of Time, will he think about space, his native land, this mother earth!

In agrarian society, man lived, loved and died for his land. Where is the native land of modern man? The soldier dies to protect his motherland. Let modern man not die without living, belonging or comprehending some years of life before it is too late with only tears, and frustration!

# Case 10

## Two Yogis

A saffron robed well built patient was admitted to our ward with breathlessness and disturbed level of consciousness. He was kept on Bed 16, a bed closest to the nurses table for good and steady observation. The head end of the bed was raised to relieve some mechanical difficulty in breathing. He was 99 years of age. Visitors poured in to see him, some were full of reverence for his 'darshan', touched his feet, others silently stood in prayer. He was a yoga-guru(Hatha-yoga), who had an organization for teaching yogasanas and pranayama to students. The yoga institution is decades old. The man had a strong physique, fair complexion. The physical frame did not seem glowing (notion is that of an aura or hallow around yogis). He was like a man who had devoted his life to a particular style of living and wore saffron clothes instead of normal colours. This was the first saffron-clad living person I saw in close range. My imagination of a sanyasi is like Swami Vivekananda, the ultimate of ethereal handsomeness in the saffron.

A medical doctor became Sri Aurobindo's disciple after returning from postgraduate medical school abroad. He was a man of moderate frame and dark brown complexion with only muscles and very little fat. He was the disciple who wrote the Guru's words when Sri Aurobindo transcended his spiritual vision to words for his epic poem "Savitri!" This disciple Nirodharan and Champaklal slept in Guru's room after Sri Aurobindo's Mahasamadhi on December 5, 1950. We met Nirodda whenever we visited Sri Aurobindo Ashram, Pondicherry. His dwelling was in a single room ten feet by four feet with belongings in the form of a cupboard for a few utensils, one bookshelf, two tables, one easy-chair two cushioned chairs, two stools, a few clothes hanging. Usually he sat with a full length loin cloth, bare body (the climate is very humid) on the easy-chair facing the Samadhi of Sri Aurobindo and the Mother.

Visitors met him in this room between 4 and 4:30 p.m. and were offered tea and biscuits readied by his niece. At ninety years of age he wore no glasses. He did not need any medication ever. His birthday was on November 17 which coincided with the passing away of the Mother and hence he stopped accepting any greetings on his birthday after 1973. Nirodda spoke very little but surely heard whatever essence he wished to. He had a keen method of filtering verbal information through hearing. When he was caught by physical ailment for the first time, he was 103 years of age. The chief medical doctor could not accept that a Yogi's physical body is not functionally similar to that of an ordinary mortal. Life of Sadhana (penance) and Tapasya (askesis) gradually purifies and transforms all layers of human being, the intellectual, the mental the vital and also the stubborn physical. Transformation is the very essence of integral yoga of Sri Aurobindo and the Mother.

Integral yoga says 'All life is yoga consciously or unconsciously.' In Sri Aurobindo's yoga there are no rules or regulations or rituals to be followed. Everyone can choose his or her own path and means. Transformation has to be achieved gradually with rejection of falsehood and ignorance, aspiration for higher and higher realms of yoga in life and total surrender to the Supreme. Simply told, most find it difficult to follow because the path is laid down and there is no compulsion whatsoever. Nirodda was with his Guru from 1932 to 1950 of which the last 12 years were in close association when he wrote down the Guru's words.

Alas ! Humanity still ill accepts such exceptional yogis. Rigid concepts of matter and body hold doctors back from accepting, leave alone realising other realms beyond. The sadhaks and devotees of Sri Aurobindo do not have any dress code so they externally appear no different to ordinary sight. The master centurian yogi was treated like a usual patient. He was unconscious so a daily medical bulletin was sent out by the treating medical doctor for information to all interested. When I visited him, 'Peace, very solid Peace' in the ambience filled my being. He seemed not a physical body but an 'Adhara', a matter base through which spiritual energy was doing work. Sri Aurobindo and the Mother's presence were in the environment, enveloping the being of their disciple. Coma is perplexing medically. Consciousness for medial purposes is divided and graded with the perspective of motor, sensory, autonomic and many brain functions. This is a rather infantile concept in respect of consciousness in spirituality where its dimensions are close to Eternity in time and to Infinity in space. Peace of the ambience was compelling for any devotee for meditation and silent reading of Savitri (an epic poem written of by Sri Aurobindo), the verbal representation of transcendental experience, every line meditation.

One could not help going back to December 5, 1950 (which we only know by reading of books) when the Master, Sri Aurobindo took Mahasamadhi, His physical body remained glowing with a golden purple hallow till December 9, 1950 during which thousands of visitors passed across with reverence, to have the last Darshan of the greatest yogi of the twentieth century, who visualized the humanity of tomorrow, transformed and supramental. Absolute Silence was maintained, without tears or overt emotional display. Imaginary visualization of the scenario speaks volumes about Immortality, Universality and Transcendental nature of the soul. In the early twentieth century this disciple was the torch bearer of the Guru's spiritual realisations. The disciples had beautiful names Amrit, Pavitra, Naloni, Champaklal, Suderam, Udar.

Immortal we are, to Immortality we travel, there is no mortality, the form only changes, life will change to Life Divine.

Thy embrace which rends the living knot of pain,
Thy joy, O Lord, in which all creatures breathe,
Thy magic flowing waters of deep love,
Thy sweetness give to me for earth and men.

**Savitri – Sri. Aurobindo**

# Epilogue

And life goes on, human beings are born like a miracle, live life doing myriad 'karma,' oblivious mostly about larger dimensions of life and existence. Only philosophers, yogis and we doctors are to care for life. Philosophers are on theoretical plane, yogis work with a few who follow them. The battlefront is faced by the medical men day in and day out, be it any season, any reason, going on and on. Every case comes as an unsolved problem, sometimes it is solved or alleviated and sometimes life ends. The metaphysical question stares us in the face as to what goes out of the body to make the living, a dead individual. "The soul is immortal" may be a metaphysical truth but what is "life" and what is "death" is enigmatic. There are parameters for judging stoppage of heart, respiration but how is the question, what was the driving force till the point of 'no return' is enigma. After more than three decades of being a medical person, I have not ceased to wonder at the miracle of new birth. I cannot stop being pensive, withdrawn, stunned after a death, not because we could not save the life but as to the cause of the phenomenon ...!

And life goes on ...! The pebbles turn to pearls!